JAMVA CHALOJI-2

MORE PARSI DELICACIES TO TICKLE YOUR PALATE

JAMVA CHALOJI - 2
MORE PARSI DELICACIES TO TICKLE YOUR PALATE

KATY DALAL

VAKILS, FEFFER AND SIMONS PVT. LTD.
Hague Building, 9, Sprott Road,
Ballard Estate, Mumbai 400 001.

First printing 2003

Price: Rs. 295/-

Published by Bimal A. Mehta for
Vakils, Feffer and Simons Pvt. Ltd., Hague Building,
9, Sprott Road, Ballard Estate, Mumbai 400 001.

Printed by Arun K. Mehta at Vakil & Sons Pvt. Ltd.,
Industry Manor, 2nd Floor, Appasaheb Marathe Marg,
Prabhadevi, Mumbai 400 025.

Colour Photographs: Arish Patel

ISBN 81-87111-64-X

This Book is dedicated

to

Feroze Dalal

A man of honesty and integrity

A man of compassion and understanding

A man to turn to for help.

May Ahura Mazda give him good health and allow him to enter Garodemane, the House of Song, when his time arrives.

CONTENTS

FISH

CHICKEN

VEGETABLES

DALS

CHUTNEY / PICKLES

AUTHOR'S FOREWORD

Jamva Chaloji – 2 is a collection of all the Parsi Recipes that could not be accommodated in the first book. It mainly consists of items which are not as commonly made as they were 50 years ago. This is because the kitchens are much smaller in towns and cities compared to the farmhouse ones, there is little or no time to devote to small luxuries such as sweet-making or vasanoo making or cooking unusual meat, chicken or fish dishes, because the mothers go to work in offices and are too strained when they return home to slog making the evening meal.

One reason why many unfamiliar recipes are included is because I felt that a collection of them was necessary. Our people should know and remember what had been cooked in their grandparents' times. Papau-ma-gos, sekta-ni-sing-per-eeda, gor-amli-na-ras-ma-patra-ni-macchi, gos-nu-stew are items no longer to be seen on Parsi tables.

Incidentally, five of the most tasty items in this book are, Tatreli-Kolmi, Bhunjeli-Marghi, Marghi-na-Tukra-nu-Achar, and Kesar-ne-Dahi-ma-randheli-Marghi and its pulao; and last, but not the least, Eeda-Paak.

Khariya-ni-Jelly and Dudh-na-Puff used to be great favourites. Do try to make the milk puffs. The jelly is another matter – very time consuming, but very tasty.

The food photographs contain sweets and savouries made in my own kitchen. However, I could not make all the sweets shown in "Sweets At Tea Time" on one and the same day. So I asked Framroze, the pastry-man at Banaji Agiary, Fort, for his help. The Mehsoor Paak and Laāl Chikkat Halwas were sent to me by Jeroo Nariman of Parsi Dairy. The Khamneli-keri-no-murabbo, the Eeda-No-Ravo and Homai Nalladaru's Mawa-no-Kopra-Paak took half a day to make. The rest of the day went in making savoury dishes for the shoot.

The first thing a cook should remember is that he or she must use ghee, chilli and masalas according to their personal tastes. Sugar should always be used carefully. Some people like sweet items and others don't like them very sweet. So you should always taste for sugar. Do not blame the recipe.

I have to thank Miss Katy Cooper of Vakils for being so kind, encouraging and helpful whilst this book was being written.

Mrs. Persis Kothawalla has my heartfelt thanks for loaning me her silver trays.

I thank Allamai Katrak and her son Rusi for all the help they extended to me during the photographing of "Muktad-nu-Bhatiyu". We have a beautiful picture of Mr. Rusi Katrak praying over the food, fruit, flowers and the "shiyav", over a golden sandalwood fire.

I thank my very dear friend Mahrukh Katrak for the numerous errands she ran for me as well as her warm support.

I wish to thank Mr. Farokh Dumasia with all my heart for the enormous help he gave me with the flower decorations and during the photographic sessions.

Last but not the least, I thank all my readers for making "Jamva Chaloji" such a great success.

Introduction

I

Today, the Parsis are a happy-go-lucky people. They enjoy their food and their festivals and by and large are economically very well off. But this was not always the case. After the last Persian Emperor Yazdezard Sheriar's Sassanian army was defeated at Nehavand in 64 A.D., the Arab rulers were merciless towards the defeated populace. It was either convert or die. In the face of terrible atrocities, those Persians, especially the ones coming from Yezd, Kerman and other Zoroastrian strongholds, decided to flee the land. They streamed across lost Sassanian lands and we are told that over 100,000 of them fled under Prince Feroze, Yezdezard's son, to China. Here, the Prince was given sanctuary by the emperor. He became a Captain in the Chinese army and built an agiary there.

Another source tells us that a number of Zoroastrians fled to Afghanistan for refuge.

But all these people gradually got amalgamated with the indigenous populations of the countries they sought refuge in.

It is only the boatloads of Parsis who came to the coast of Sanjan in Gujarat, who survived – and are yet in existence after 1300 years. Persia and India have a long historical connection from the times of Cyrus and Darius, who ruled over the Punjab and received as annual tribute, 300,000 talents of gold. Under the Sassanians, there was even more interaction. We are reliably told that one of the daughters of Yezdezard Sheriar was married to a Prince of Mewar, whilst the Sassanian King Behramgore came to hunt wild oxen in the Rann of Cutch, and in the process married an Indian princess, Sapinuda.

The Parsis came as refugees and were given asylum by the ruler of Sanjan. To this day, nobody can say with authority who he was, but Parsi tradition calls him Jadav Rana.

There was tremendous traffic between Persia and China, along the Silk Route. For the first time, at excavations in Sanjan, we have discovered the remains of Sassanian Pottery in India. Sanjan, from the explorations carried out, appears to have been a large port or bunder, 1500 years ago. If Parsis knew of Sanjan through their trade, then it is extremely reasonable to believe that they set out by sea from Persia to find sanctuary on Indian soil.

One of the greatest tragedies of the ancient Persians who came to India is the paucity of written records. Unlike the Greeks who wrote vast accounts of what they saw and heard, we have no written history to fall back upon. The inscription of Darius at Behistun gives us a glimpse, for the first time into the lives of the ancient Achaemenids. We have to fall back on the Greeks, primarily Herodotus, for our accounts. He never travelled to Persia himself. His history was based on the accounts of Egyptian priests who hated Cambyses, the son of Cyrus, for conquering their country. For 2500 years, the world subscribed to the lies of Herodotus and the Egyptians.

If the Persians had written their own accounts, unjustified vilification would not have taken place.

Dearth of ancient Persian written records and Parsi history in India have cost us dear.

II

Mani Kamerkar and Soonu Dhunjishaw have written an excellent book called "From the Iranian Plateau To the Shores of Gujarat", in which they have managed to collect almost all the information available regarding the Parsis after their landing at Sanjan.

There is one tragic event that they have missed out which I would like all our Parsi friends to know and ponder over. Things were not always easy for our people and we have some stray evidence from here and there that we can put together to draw a picture of the past. The old "Naam-Garan" books tell us of the death dates of a number of important people. It is from these old M.S.S. that we first got to know the names of Dasturan Dastur Meherji Rana's family.

On the 25th day i.e. Ashishwang of the 1st month Farvardin, a massacre of Parsis took place along the Tapti river. The people belonged to the settlement of Variav which, according to one account, was as old as Sanjan.

This event is referred to in the Bombay Gazetteer as well as the History of Naosari written by S. M. Desai. Kharsedji Nusserwanji Seervai and Khan Bahadur Bomanji Byramji Patel have also referred to the massacre in their article on "Gujarat Parsees" in the Bombay Gazetteer.

Amongst us Parsis, the 25th day of Mah Farvardin, this event is remembered as "Variav Behdinonu Parabh". Unfortunately, we do not know the year in which this event occurred. But, for several hundred years, this day is recognized as a sad day on which the deaths of these Variav Behdins is commemorated.

One account says that because the Parsis did not pay "tribute" to the Rajput Chief of Ratanpur, he sent forces to enforce his order. The Parsi men of the settlement were enjoying a festival in their faraway fields, happily wining and dining. There were only women left at home. The brave women put on male armour and very bravely faced the enemy. Sad to say, they were on the point of driving away the enemy, when one of the females lost her metal helmet and her hair streamed free in the breeze. Upon seeing this, the males rallied and made a terrible assault on the women who "preferring death to dishonour, heroically leapt into the Tapti."

The second account tells us that after the Parsi arrival in Sanjan, a great number of them settled at Variav which was situated in Kamrej Taluka. A great number of Bhils lived in this area. These Bhils used to harrass the Parsi farmers and frequently looted their settlement. One day, all the Parsi men went into their fields to celebrate some festival and there was heavy eating and drinking. Taking advantage of this, the Bhils crept into the Variav settlement. Helpless, the brave women donned the armour of their male relatives and set out to meet the enemy. At first all went well, and the Bhils were about to retreat, when one of the women lost her helmet or it became askew because it may have been loose on her head. Her long hair streamed out in the wind. Seeing this, the Bhils, ashamed of their near defeat, got a second wind and rushed against the hapless women. Merciless killing and looting of armour ensued. The Parsi men, lolling after a happy, heavy meal, were slaughtered in the fields where they lay in a somnolent doze. The few who escaped ran away to Navsari and their descendants have been living ever since in a place called Malesar Falia or Malesar Street.

All the dead are revered together in one prayer. Nobody knows who died where. Baj and Farokshi prayers have been said on this day for several hundred years.

An old "Naam-Garan" book, over 200 years old, also refers to this event.

Many people living in Malesar have the baj-rozgar done on their own. Those who cannot afford the money, attend the Anjuman prayers.

East of Lunsikooi, there is a famous place called "Dashera Tekdi" or Hill. There used to exist a giant banyan tree there. Many religious ceremonies were carried out at this place and the old tree was called "Ghambariyo Vad". This was a meeting place where the people of Navsari took many important decisions regarding their lives.

On Ashishwang Roz, Mah Farvardin, over 500 people used to gather here and take part in the "Hamajor" prayers. Till today, this ceremony is held in this place with great respect and reverence. The area was large, almost 19 bighas and belonged to the Parsi community. Once the local Mohammedans and then the Gaikwad government tried to take it away from them. Both efforts were fruitless.

After the Baj and Farokshi prayers were over, everyone, old and young, who had assembled there, were fed with a chasni of deliciously cooked vaal (beans) and rotlis and liquor was freely distributed – not any more now, because of prohibition.

I asked Dr. Feroze Kotwal about this event and he had said that he had participated in this event as a young boy and also eaten the beans and rotli.

God bless the souls of the dead of Variav!

III

After the Maratha victory at the Battle of Bassein, the region around Sanjan came under the rule of the Peshwa. It was the Peshwa's aim to make the region productive and he, therefore, made available to agriculturists vast tracts of hitherto unused virgin forest lands.

The Parsis in the vicinity rose to the occasion and took up the challenge of turning the forests into farmlands. Large acres were brought under the plough and the choice of crop surprisingly was rice. Rice is essentially a subsistence crop and not a cash crop in this region. The Parsis overcame this hurdle by mass-cultivating rice. To achieve this, an enormous area had to be cultivated. Parsi land holdings of 15,000 acres were common. The largest, held by the Karbhari family, was 40,000 acres. Local legend has it that Mr. Karbhari built himself a town (Udhwa) so as to provide a ready market yard for the produce from his lands.

Besides rice, grass and wood were also major produces of the region. Whereas grass was consumed locally, wood was exported from the region by sea from Umargaon via Sanjan. Minor produce included fruits, toddy, liquor and pulses. The Parsis who hailed from coastal settlements like Gholwad, Bordi, Jhai, Govada, Davier, and Nargol, built large farmhouses on their lands to serve as home away from home.

The Zoroastrian families lived miles away from each other. The wives and children lived in the villages of Sanjan, Nargol, Saronda, whilst the men lived in their homes in the jungles. There was very little time to exchange news. Many families lived on the coast as well and the families were widely scattered; hence, there was very little social intermingling of the entire community at a single venue. To facilitate such a gathering, the inhabitants of the area decided (around about 1920), to hold an annual ghambhar in memory of each year's dead, and a celebration of the living. This function was held in rotation at various far-flung farms and was held under the auspices of the "Junglewasi Ghambhar Committee". The food was free and people came from Umargaon to Davier. In fact, nowadays, they even come from Bombay. My son, Kurush, once catered for the Ghambhar. He was provided all the provisions, chicken and other things by the Committee and fed 500 people at Surungi and 800 people at the Davier Dadgah's Salgirah celebrations.

The traditional food at these Ghambhars was:

    Istoo

    Papeta ma Gos/Murghi

    Dhansakh Dal

    Brown Rice

    Kachumber

But at the Salgirah, the Brown Rice is substituted by Pullao or the Dal/Rice by Dhan Dar Patiyo.

They were large-hearted men, these grand old farmers and marched like giants across the pages of Sanjan's history. They helped their brethren unstintingly in their hours of need.

We have a few such names still buried in our hearts. They are Khan Bahadur Dinshaji Davierwalla, Barrister Homi Davierwalla, our present friend Rohinton Davierwalla, Maneckshaw Vervadewalla, and the most illustrious of them all, Khan Bahadur Dinshaji Wadia, who was an M.B.E. or Member of the British Empire, which was a title given by the King Emperor. The titles Khan Saheb and Khan Bahadur were given by the Viceroy of India. I remember Bawaji, my great-grandfather, Kanjibhai Patel, once went from Tadgaon to Sanjan to buy some wood from Dinshaji Wadia. The grand old man told him to take whatsoever he needed – free of cost.

Munchershaw Davierwalla was an M.L.A. of the area.

The Independence of India, although cheered by Parsis, acted as a death knell to Parsi fortunes. The mighty were humbled by one stroke of the pen. There were three reasons for this:

1. *Prohibition marked the end of these rich Parsis because their major businesses were toddy and liquor. At one stroke, they lost their main businesses.*

2. *The other reason was the Tenancy Act, according to which, their ancestral lands had to be sold to their tenants at a ridiculously low price. Added to this by virtue of the Land Ceiling Act, the government acquired the surplus lands at very low prices.*

3. *Some Parsis had their own Bus Transport Services. They lost this business due to the formation of the State Transport, which nationalized the bus services.*

My sincere thanks to Dr. Kurush Dalal and Mr. Jehan Wadia for the above information.

IV

A MAN AMONGST MEN

I knew a man, when I was a child, living near Sanjan, who grew from abject poverty to riches and became in his own lifetime, the wealthiest man in the huge area between Sanjan and Bhilad. His name was Sorabji Balsara, of Mamakwada – popularly known as Valsara Fooa.

As a child of 7, I had once been taken over to his house in an oxen cart. We – that is my great-grandfather's family – were invited for lunch. As we were on holiday at Tadgaon, mother and I were included in the invitation. Till this day, I have never forgotten the sight of his dining tables, groaning with the choicest of foods. There was chicken, mutton, fish and rice. What I particularly remember is a huge, shallow, high-sided terracotta dish filled with curds, whose surface was decorated by red chilli powder in a trellis design. When I began to write this book, I contacted Wing Cmdr. Hoshang Patel and his sister Silloo Vaid, and came upon some interesting data regarding Valsara Fooa.

He began life as a clever, energetic but a very poor man. Behramji Patel, a rich landowner of Tadgaon, my great-grandfather Kanjibhai's father, happened to see him and appreciated what he saw. He promised the young man that he would give him a place near his jungles on rent if he married his second daughter, Allibai.

So, Sorabji married the young maiden and went to live on his land where he built a shack or jhopra and his 3 children were all born in it. Times were very bad and it is said that there was no "nimak" to put in the dhan (rice). Allibai died at an early age. After a short gap, Sorabji went to Daman to marry her sister Gulli, who had become a widow. He brought her and her 3 children to Mamakwada. Slowly, his luck turned and his future became brighter and brighter. During the First World War period 1914-1918, he came into contact with a rich landowner called, Bhiladwalla. This gentleman gave Sorabji contracts for grass cutting and for the hiring of labourers. He slowly became a very rich man in his own stead.

Unfortunately, Bhiladwalla fell upon bad days and could not pay Sorabji the money he owed him. So instead of cash, he gave him a godown in lieu of it. Sorabji built another godown next to the first one outside Bhilad Railway Station.

As he became rich, he became pious and philanthropical. Whenever he heard that any poor Parsi girl in the area of Sanjan was to be married, he paid the cost of her marriage clothes and dowry, which consisted of furniture and vessels of all sorts.

If he heard that some poor woman had been widowed, after the Charum ceremony on the 4th day, he would send her provisions of dal, rice, and tamarind, sufficient for one whole year. He would also send her wood for cooking which would suffice her for a year!! All this was done quietly without any fanfare.

He sent the foodstuffs and wood at about midnight when no one was about, with instructions to keep quiet about it all.

According to Silloo, he wrote his own songs and sang them. He was also a very good cook.

Parsi children had to go to a Municipal School. There was no proper education for them. Lady Navajbai Ratan Tata was brought down to Nargol by Rustomji Talyerkhan, to show her the village and the Tata-Wadia School which had been recently constructed.

Talyerkhan had come across Sorabji and was very impressed by his personality. Silloo says, "Bawaji" was tall, dignified, always wore a red velvet Parsi cap, and white "patloon and dagla", and travelled in a tonga driven by two spirited horses. Only the very rich had horse drawn tongas. My poor great-grandfather travelled in oxen drawn, covered carts called "galdis".

Sorabji gave loans to poor people and never ever asked anyone back for his money. If someone returned him his money, he accepted it gratefully.

So when Lady Navajbai came to Nargol, Rustomji asked "Valsara Fooa" if he could bring her to Mamakwada for lunch. He wanted her to taste the typical Parsi food cooked in the area. Of course, Sorabji was only too willing and happy to oblige.

With the help of his sister Rudibai, he prepared a grand lunch which he cooked himself. He went at 4 a.m. the day of the lunch party to Maroli, miles away, to arrange for huge lobsters and bois, which were fried, and brought direct to the table. There was chicken bhujan made out of boneless chicken, then there was "gos-no-batero" cooked in fresh toddy. The table was loaded with home-made butter, dahi, fried sev and rice chapattis. He served kolam rice grown in his own fields.

Lady Navajbai Tata and her entourage left Mamakwada, replete and happy.

Many, many years later, Sorabji's daughter Khorshedbanoo Patel, happened to see Navajbai in 1952 at the marriage of Jimmy Mehta and Shapoorji Pallonji's daughter. She immediately recognized Khorshedbanoo and came over to her and asked, "Aren't you Sorabji Balsara's daughter?" Then, she carried on to say, "I have never eaten such delicious food as I did at Mamakwada. I still remember it."

The old man died at 84 years of age. Chaos set in. His wife emptied the house of all possessions and walked out because Fooa had left the farm to Allibai's eldest son, Rustam. He had provided magnificently for Gullibai in gold and cash and land. But nothing was enough for her. It was the end of a beautiful dream. The large estate was sold for not even 1/10th its value, and there are only memories left of Mamakwada's glory.

V

THE PARSIS AND THEIR USE OF SUGARCANE VINEGAR

The Parsis must be the only community in India to use such a vast amount of vinegar in their foodstuffs and pickles.

In days gone by, food would turn bad very quickly, especially in the hot season in Gujarat. To preserve cooked food, many of our daily food items also included vinegar. For instance, fresh fish patias, different sahas were dependent on vinegar *for their sweet-sour taste. Mango, carrot and dried fruit chutneys used vinegar. The most famous item was dried Bombay Duck patia which was cooked in pure vinegar without a drop of water, so it could stay like a pickle. Soonamai made boomla-no-patio of 200 dried Bombay Ducks at a time, and then put it in terracotta pots and hung them from the ceiling in "sikkas" made out of rope.*

Today, every Parsi who buys vinegar uses E.F. Kolah's vinegar or Kershasp Kolah's vinegar, which is made in Navsari. I get mine from Yezd who is the great grandson of E.F. Kolah. In 1885, it was a small concern and vinegar was packed in earthenware jars. Later on the vinegar was packed in wooden casks or barrels. The sugarcane juice was obtained from the village of Mora in Navsari Taluka. Today, the factory which was originally in the city, is on the highway.

The manufacturing process remains the same, all made in the traditional method.

Once the juice is fermented, it turns into ethyl alcohol. If matured further, aceto-bacteria take over. After maturing, it is filtered and transferred into containers. This transferring and filtering and exposure to natural environments, improves the texture of the vinegar. The Kolahs use no additives.

Some years ago, they used to send me vinegar in giant plastic drums. Nowadays, I receive it in plastic pouches.

VI

A SMALL NOTE ON TODDY

Toddy or "tadi" is the mildly fermented sap of the date palm commonly known as "khajuri". Its Latin name is 'dactylifera sp.' The sap is collected by making a deep incision in the crown of the plant very close to the apical or central stem. The sap flows along a deep 'V' shaped incision into a terracotta or clay pot called "ghariyu" tied immediately under the crown.

These pots are emptied every morning and in rare cases every evening. The toddy rapidly ferments in sunlight and therefore is usually removed and sold early in the morning. Younger, shorter trees produce more toddy than older, taller trees. The yield of toddy is commercially viable only for a period of 2 to 3 months a year, after which it needs to be rested for a year. Neera is a non-alcoholic version of toddy. In this case, the pots are tied to the tree at night and are removed prior to sunrise, so as to prevent fermentation. The cut for neera is deeper and most trees need to be rested for 2 to 3 years before they can be re-used.

Toddy, sold early in the morning, is called sweet toddy and is considered highly beneficial. The toddy sold in the evenings is called sour toddy, and is essentially consumed for its intoxicating properties. Date trees which are tapped for toddy do not yield any fruits.

The Parsi farmer's life was wrapped around his toddy trees. He grew rich on them. They brought him a good income. He used toddy in some food as well as sweet dishes such as bhakras and popatjees.

When the prohibition to toddy tapping was announced by the government after the 1947 independence, thousands of Parsis who were involved in the toddy and liquor business, were ruined. Overnight disaster struck them. This unexpected blow brought 95% of the toddy farmers to their knees and made them helpless, disoriented and jobless.

Their lands were taken away from them. The government rule was "khede teni zamin". The land belonged to the one who tilled it. So, all the land which was given to the "kul" or servants to till so that they gave part of the yield to the seth, became the possession of the servants or the tillers. The rule said only 35 acres could be held by one person. Most of the farms crumbled up and owners were left dry-eyed and defeated.

So, there was an exodus from the country of young people who left their homes in search of jobs and a better education. The homes in Parsi villages started showing locks on the front doors and many happy villages slowly began to fade and become ghost towns.

The end of toddy tapping was practically the end of the Parsi farmer. A new chapter began for him in the cities of Bombay, Ahmedabad, Surat, Bharuch, Ankleshwar, Vapi, Valsad and others.

VII

A NOTE ON THE EXCAVATIONS AT SANJAN

The World Zarthushti Cultural Foundation under Dr. Homi Dhalla and Dr. Mani Kamerkar, undertook a survey of the Sanjan region and have excavated at Sanjan for two reasons. The resulting finds were very dramatic. The excavations prove that

Sanjan was occupied by the Satavahanas and the Western Kshatrapas during the 1st and 2nd century A.D. For the first time, we have found Sassanid remains in India going back to the 7th and 8th century A.D. which include part of a silver coin. About 1200 iron and glass artifacts, beads and pendants and decorated vessel fragments have been found. But most important is the turquoise glazed ware called Sassanian Islamic glazed ware, which was found. This shows close connections between Iran and India in the 6th to 8th centuries A.D. The Iranian Zarthushtrians came by sea to Gujarat where they already had trade links.

Dr. S.P. Gupta, Chairman of the Indian Archaeological Society, New Delhi, has helped the ZSCF carry out surveys at the Bahrot Caves where the holy fire was kept hidden for 12 years after Sanjan was ransacked around 1373 A.D. by Sultan Mahmud Shah Tughluq's General, Alaf Khan.

The Government of India has accepted the WZCF's request to make Bahrot a national monument. What is needed is to build a pathway upto the caves, which are in a poor condition.

Funds are urgently required for Bahrot, at least 40 lakhs of rupees will be needed! The excavations need money desperately.

If we do not protect these old caves and gather more information at the Sanjan site, we will lose our last opportunity to know something of our past.

JAMSHEDI NAVROZE CELEBRATIONS

Once the securities of the villages of Gujarat were left behind, half a century ago, the Parsi became a changed phenomenon. Life in the cities was full of tension. Time became the most important thing in their lives. There was little or no leisure time. Men and women went to work. Their days revolved around buses and trains to catch. The adults had to be in time in their offices. The children had to rush to school.

The days of leisurely breakfasts were over. Lunch was made up of biscuit packets, wafers or sandwiches. The lady of the house, after a hectic day at the office, had to return and cook dinner and catch up on household chores. Life became an eternal rush. There was just no time for morning prayers, except for a hurried kusti. The morning and evening sukhar-lobaan *ritual became a thing of the past. If the family was lucky and there was a grandmother living with them, she saw to the daily* diva *and that the* sukhar-lobaan *was wafted throughout the house, twice a day. It was she who saw to it that the servant washed the "umbers" daily and put "chowk" on them and that torans were put on the doors on all "hamkaras" or Ahuramazda, Ardibehest, Behram, Adar and Ashishwang Roz, on all "parabhs", Adar Mahino and Adar Roz, etc. etc.*

When I was a child, Jamshedi Navroze, Khordad Sal (the prophet's birthday) and diso or death day, were all Public Holidays. So the whole family participated in the prayers and the partying.

Jamshedi Navroze is the Spring Equinox on 21st of March, which Zoroastrians all over the world celebrate with great gusto.

The morning began with everybody in the family rushing through their baths and donning new clothes from head to toe. Even the very poor Parsis saw to it that their children wore new sadra-kusti, topi and sapat.

Breakfast was a dream. You had sev or rawa, boiled eggs and yellow bananas and the same were sent to the neighbours' houses, along with "sakar" and "nariel". I remember my grandmother and mother making a luscious rawa with saffron and eggs and sending it next door to my friend, Jeroo Dastur, and her landlady, Roda Bamji.

Lunch was partaken of when everybody returned from the agiary. My Bapaiji and Mama would, of course, be busy preparing lunch which would consist of mutton khurma or dahiwalli marghi, pulao made with mutton and fried potato chunks, covered lavishly with kismis and badam. The whole meal was followed by tall glasses of falooda, topped with white or pink icecream and malai.

Most of us know that the falooda is made of tukmuria seeds, rose sherbet, sweetened milk and icecream, but very few people know that the most important part of the falooda was the "ghehu-nu-dudh-na-biyan" or "beej".

Making wheat milk or ghehu-nu-dudh was one of the most tedious processes of my young life. I remember everything very clearly. The best of wheat was bought from the bania and cleaned and soaked in a huge kalai tapeli. Every day, the wheat was soaked in clean water until the day when you pressed a grain between your fingers and a milky pulp popped out. Then, the wheat was washed and the water drained and the softened wheat was put through a meat mincing machine, twice over. The milk was separated from the coarse shell of the wheat, which was discarded. The mincing process included a lot of water being used. So, the wheat-milk was allowed to stand till the water floated above the milk. The water was slowly discarded until only the thick milk remained.

Two shallow baskets were prepared. They were filled three-fourths with ash. Then the ash was covered with newspapers upto a thickness of half an inch. Over the newspapers, several thicknesses of muslin or mulmul was laid. Finally, on top of it all, the thick milk was poured. Then the basket was kept in the hot sun on the terrace for days until the milk became thick and solid and dry as brick. Then, it was removed from the basket in pieces. The thick brown skin which had formed on the top of the milk was removed. The pieces were again put in the thalas to become crisp. Once the crisp stage was reached, the milk was stored in large airtight glass bottles.

When Jamshedi Navroze was around the corner, friends and relatives would come to buy Mama's ghehu-nu-dudh. They said that the milk was whiter than that which was sold in the shops and did not smell peculiar like the bania's milk.

The making of the "biyan" or "beej" meaning seed, was the most difficult part of making the falooda.

One day before the falooda was to be had, "tukmuria" seeds were cleaned and soaked in a vessel of water. The next day you would find that the black seeds had swollen and were surrounded by a white jelly-like substance.

To make the wheat milk, you need 2 people, 2 large vessels, 1 kalai-nu-boiyyu or sieve and a lot of ice, some sugar, and "golab-nu-pani" or rose water.

Half a kilo of the milk is broken up into little crumbs and soaked in 2-3 litres of water. When the milk has softened, it is mixed vigorously in the water and placed on a high flame and stirred continuously till the water evaporates and the mixture becomes thick. Add a little sugar and some rose water and keep mixing until it is stiff like a dough. Remove from the fire.

Place the sieve on top of a vessel filled with broken ice. Take a "kucchi" or a ladle, and put the milk a little at a time and pass it through the sieve. Little drops or seeds will fall on the ice and float in its icy water. If the mixture is not firm, the seeds will disintegrate. Keep the ice water with the seeds in the refrigerator so that the seeds remain firm.

Heat 3 litres of full cream milk with 3 cups of sugar and bring to a boil 4 times. Cool. Place in the refrigerator and chill till needed. Also, order some malai, at least 750 gms. and chill it.

When it is time to serve the falooda, arrange 12 tall glasses in a tray. Place one tablespoon of tukmuria seeds at the bottom of each glass, then add 1" of rose sherbet on top of it. Add 2 tablespoons of wheat milk seeds and then pour the chilled milk into each glass, till the glass is three-quarters full. Top with a large scoop of strawberry pink or white vanilla icecream and malai. Serve each glass on a bone china quarter plate with a long spoon in it.

NAVROZE-NO-PULAO

(Navroze Day Pulao)

For the Rice:

1 kg. Basmati rice
1½ gms. pure Spanish saffron
    (if possible)
6 green cardamoms, bruised lightly
2 1" piece cinnamon
2 star anise
4 mace flowers
3 deep fried onions
Salt
½ cup pure ghee

For the Mutton:

1 kg. 500 gms. mutton
4 large onions, finely chopped
400 gms. thick creamy curds
1½ tbsps. ginger-garlic paste
1 gm. saffron
Pure ghee

Masala for the Potli:

20 black peppercorns,
    broiled
10 Kashmiri chillies,
    broiled
4 cloves, broiled
10 mace flowers,
    broiled
3 star anise, broiled
1 tsp. shahjeera, broiled
½ tsp. caraway seeds,
    broiled

Grind very coarsely and tie in a piece of muslin cloth to which a 2 ft. string is tied

Preparation time	:	20-25 mins.
Cooking time	:	2 hours
Serves	:	10-12

Method for the Rice:

- Place the washed rice in the electric rice cooker.

- Heat the saffron lightly on a tava. When crisp, dissolve it in ½ cup of hot water and crumble it with your fingers. Add to the rice.

- Add the cardamoms, cinnamon, star anise, mace, deep fried onions, salt, ghee and sufficient water to the rice and allow to cook till tender.

Method for the Mutton and the use of the Potli:

- Add salt and the ginger-garlic paste to the mutton.

- Whisk the curds with a pinch of salt and pour it over the mutton. Keep aside for 2 hours.

- Place ¾ cup of pure ghee in a large tapeli and cook the finely chopped onions till golden-pink and soft. Then add the marinated mutton and allow to simmer in its own juice for 10 minutes. Meanwhile, heat the saffron and add it to the mutton, exactly as you added it to the rice.

- Now pick up the potli and with the help of the string attached to it, place it on the cooking mutton as soon as the 10 minutes for cooking the meat are up. Add 3 to 4 cups of water and allow the mutton to simmer for 1½ hours. Be sure to place a weight on the string so that it does not fall into the tapeli. Cover tightly with a lid, and add water on top of the lid, and cook till the mutton is tender. Stir every 20 minutes and check to see that the mutton does not burn and add the hot water on the lid replenishing it as often as you use it.

- Once the mutton is tender, lift up the potli, squeeze any juice it contains into the mutton-tapeli and discard it.

Dry Fruits for the Pulao:

20 apricots, soaked overnight in
   sugar water
150 gms. very large Irani dried
   raisins, deseeded
   and lightly fried
100 gms. large almonds, boiled,
   skinned and fried

For the Decoration:

12 boiled eggs, cut into half
25 gms. boiled, skinned and finely
   sliced pistachios
The petals of 2 pink roses, dipped
   in syrup and then dried in a slow
   oven or in the sun
$1/3$rd of the white rice
4 drops cochineal
20 boiled, skinned and fried almonds
2 deep fried onions

To Lay Out the Pulao:

- Take a large clean tapeli and smear its bottom with a little ghee.

- Place ½ the rice in the tapeli. Then place all the mutton on top of it. Cover it with the apricots, the large raisins and the fried almonds. Then top it up with all the remaining rice. Seal the mouth with foil and aata or dough.

- Place the tapeli on a tava which is placed on a medium heat for 25 minutes.

- Serve the pulao on a silver dish. Remove it with a quarter plate and lift out the mutton and rice from deep inside the tapeli. Top with the rose petals in the centre of the dish. On either side place the reserved white rice which should be mixed with the drops of cochineal mixed into ½ cup of lukewarm water. Cover the pink rice with the whole fried almonds and decorate the edges of the pulao with a circle of boiled eggs cut into halves or slices and a circle of deep fried onions.

- Serve with sweet curds, dhansakh dal, and a green salad made up of fresh pineapple rings, lettuce, cucumber and sliced onions, with a lime-sugar and coriander seed dressing.

NAVROZE-NO-KHURMO
(Navroze Day Special Khurma)

2 kgs. mutton leg chunks with nali
2 tbsps. ginger-garlic paste
4 large onions, finely chopped

Masala No. 1

20 black peppercorns
10 Kashmiri chillies
5 cloves
2" cinnamon
Seeds of 5 green
   cardamoms
1 tbsp. fennel seeds
1 tsp. shahjeera
6 mace flowers

} Lightly broil and grind fine

Masala No. 2

100 gms. kismis
50 gms. almonds
50 gms. cashew nuts
50 gms. pistachios
1-2 gms. saffron

} Grind fine in a little water till soft and buttery

8 potatoes, skinned and each cut
   into 8 pieces and soaked in salted
   water
Salt
Ghee

Preparation time	:	25 mins.
Cooking time	:	1½ hours
Serves	:	10-15

- Marinade the mutton in salt and ginger-garlic paste for 2 hours.

- Chop the onions and cook in ½ cup of pure ghee in a large patia. Cook the onions till golden-brown and then add the powdered masala No. 1. Stir for 3 minutes and then add the mutton and stir for 5 minutes. Then add 6 cups of water and place on a slow fire till the mutton is soft and tender and very little water is left.

- Make a hole in the center of the tapeli and put in the masala No. 2 and gently mix into the cooked khurma and allow to simmer for 10 minutes.

- Half fill a karahi with oil. Place on a medium heat and when hot, put in the potatoes, a few at a time, and fry till golden red.

- Taste the khurma for salt. Serve hot, covered by the fried potatoes.

- Serve with hot rotlis, parathas or brun pao.

Forgotten Recipes

VASANOO

Vasanoo is not difficult to make. However, recipes for it are complicated. Let me explain it this way. It is a breakfast food made in the cold weather and eaten from November to February. It was thought by our great-grandmothers, to be health-giving and nutritious. Come November, in the olden days, the elderly women in each family would get together and pore over old hand-written exercise books. Then the items would be set down on note paper and sent to the dry-fruit dealer who would send all the items packed separately with the names of the contents written on brown paper bags.

Dilojan Ghadiali was Feroze's great-grandmother and was considered a great expert in the making of "Vasanoo", also called "Udadiyu", because it contained "urad-ni-dar".

It was a heavy sweet, redolent of spices such as nutmeg and cardamom (elchi-jaiphal) and mace (javintri). It was made up of 32 separate items. The most important of these were almonds, pistachios, cashew nuts, charoli, raisins, red pumpkin seeds, watermelon seeds, cucumber seeds and white gourd seeds. Dried dates, water chestnuts, lotus stems, wheat milk, various other seeds, gum, gram flour, urad flour, dried ginger and many more items, were fried, ground and cooked in pure ghee and sugar syrup.

I remember seeing Dilojan's eldest daughter, Pillamasi Icchaporia, about 36 years ago, sitting in a chair in the kitchen supervising the making of vasanoo. A huge quantity – about 28 kgs. was cooked and then distributed to the family members, according to their requests.

When I started writing this book, I asked Pillamasi's daughter-in-law, Tehmi Icchaporia for the recipe. She gave it to me cut down to one-fourth the amount.

Today, many Parsis buy this delicious sweet from the few who still make it. It costs between Rs. 250 to Rs. 350 per kilogram.

The items were fried over a medium heat in a very large patia or langri.

The syrup was made in a huge tapeli.

DILOJAN'S VASANOO RECIPE

Items to be fried and ground:

250 gms. almonds
150 gms. pistachios
200 gms. raisins
250 gms. charoli
300 gms. cashew nuts
200 gms. each 4 types of magaz or seeds of the cucumber, melon, watermelon and pumpkin
200 gms. kharak or dried dates
200 gms. singora or dried water chestnuts
125 gms. kammarkakdi or lotus stems
125 gms. gokhru
200 gms. 'gehu-nu-dudh' or wheat milk powder
125 gms. khaskhas, or poppy seeds
125 gms. dried kopra
125 gms. suva or dill seeds
125 gms. 'gunder' or gum
200 gms. urad dar aata
200 gms. chana or gram aata
1-2 kgs. pure ghee
2½ kgs. sugar
2½ karasiya or lota water

Not to be fried, but only powdered:

300 gms. dry ginger powder
10 gms. white pepper powder
15 gms. piprimul-na-gathia
10 gms. salam
10 gms. safed musli
10 gms. kali musli
10 gms. green cardamom seeds
10 gms. javintri or mace
2 pieces whole nutmegs

- Wash the raisins and allow to dry.

- Boil, skin and fry the almonds and pistachios. Grind them separately.

- Each item listed under "to be fried and ground" must be separately ground and placed in a large thali.

- The cashew nuts, charoli and the 4 magaz or vegetable seeds, are to be fried and ground separately. The same is done with the water chestnuts, wheat milk, urad dar and chana dar attas. Fry the gum last, and add ½ cup of water and keep it in a warm place.

- Boil the sugar and water in a large tapeli and cook the syrup till it becomes sticky.

- When the syrup comes to a strong boil, add the fried items, one at a time, and stir vigorously non-stop. Lower the flame.

- Then add the ground items which did not have to be fried and stir the whole mixture with a strong chamach or perforated spoon.

- Keep stirring for 25 minutes more.

- Remove from the fire when the ghee separates from the sweet.

- Pour into square aluminium trays and allow to cool overnight.

- By next morning, the extra ghee will have risen to the surface. Cut into large squares.

- Keep the vasanoo in airtight containers. Staying capacity is very good.

DHUN MASTER'S VASANOO

Behroze Burjorji has very kindly given me her mother, Dhun Master's recipe for Vasanoo. I made the vasanoo because it is for an unusually small quantity, unlike others, which have to be made from 5 to 15 kilograms at a time.

This vasanoo is excellent in taste in spite of not having 8 of the items, which we find in most vasanoos. There is an absence of fatty contents. I feel that there is a conscious effort made to keep it less greasy than the normal vasanoo we eat because, even the ghee content is very sparing. This recipe does not contain pistachios, charoli, raisins, dried dates or kharak, urad dar atta, chana aata, kali musli and dholi musli. And yet, all said and done, the taste is excellent.

When I made this vasanoo, I could not resist adding 200 gms. pistachios, 200 gms. cashew nuts, 200 gms. raisins and 100 gms. sugar. I also felt the need of 300 gms. of extra ghee, but this is personal and today's Parsis may want to eat the vasanoo exactly as it is in the original Dhun Master recipe.

1 kg. sugar
500 gms. pure ghee
250 gms. almonds, boiled, skinned
250 gms. 4-types of magaz (pumpkin, cucumber, watermelon and white pumpkin seeds)
125 gms. kammar kakdi (lotus stems)
125 gms. ghehu-nu-dudh (wheat milk)
125 gms. singora (dried water chestnuts)
50 gms. suva (dill)
50 gms. gunder (gum)
25 gms. khaskhas (poppy seeds)
25 gms. gokhru
10 gms. Punjabi salan

To be fried and ground

125 gms. dried ginger powder
30 gms. pipri-mul-na-gathia
30 gms. white peppercorns, powdered
15 gms. green cardamoms, powdered
2 whole nutmegs, powdered

- Fry all the ingredients separately and place in a thali. Then, grind them and set aside.

- Once the gum is fried, add ½ cup of water to it and set it aside in a warm place.

- Take a large, wide-mouthed vessel, a patia or langri. Add 6 cups of water and the sugar, and heat over a low fire, stirring it all the while until you get a sticky syrup. This should take about 20 minutes.

- Add all the fried stuff which has been ground and keep stirring it over a low fire until the ghee seeps out at the sides of the vessel. Now, sprinkle ginger powder, white pepper powder and the piprimul-na-gathia. Keep stirring vigorously non-stop. Lower the flame. Keep stirring until all the ghee comes to the surface. Now sprinkle the cardamom and nutmeg powders. Take the vessel off the fire.

- Pour the thick mixture into a square tray. Allow to cool. Next day, cut the vasanoo into the required pieces and place in an airtight container.

BEHRAM, GOSASP & MANIJEH MEHTA'S VASANOO

This is one of the nicest vasanoos I have ever eaten. Behram, Gosasp and Manijeh make it on a commercial basis. If you ever want to eat some, phone them up at 22842306. They live in Cusrow Baug.

1 kg. to 500 gms. sugar
1 kg. pure ghee
100 gms. almonds
100 gms. pistachios — All these
100 gms. charoli — should be
100 gms. walnuts — coarsely
200 gms. cashew nuts — ground
200 gms. 4-types of magaz
    (pumpkin, cucumber,
    white pumpkin and
    watermelon seeds)

125 gms. singora
    (water chestnuts)
50 gms. kammar kakdi
    (lotus stems)
25 gms. gokhru
100 gms. ghehu-nu-dudh — To be
    (wheat milk) — fried and
½ coconut, dried kopra vati — ground
50 gms. suva (dill) — fine
50 gms. khaskhas
    (poppy seeds)
50 gms. gunder (gum)
100 gms. urad dar
100 gms. chana dar

300 gms. soonth (ginger powder)
5 gms. safed mari (white
    pepper powder)
5 gms. piprimul-na-gathia
5 gms. lindi piper
5 gms. salam
5 gms. safed musli
5 gms. kari musli
5 gms. elchi
    (cardamom seeds) — Grind
1 whole jaiphal (nutmeg) — together
5 gms. javintri (mace)

- Proceed exactly as given in Dilojan's recipe.
- Use 3 to 4 cups water whilst making the syrup.

EDA-PAAK OR EGG HALWA

This is one of the most delicious sweets I have ever eaten and I request all my readers to make it at least once in their lifetime. The measurements in this recipe are my own. You will get 6 kgs. 100 gms. of eda paak, which is not easily available on sale, if you try this recipe.

50 egg yolks
500 gms. almonds, boiled and skinned ⎤
150 gms. pistachios, boiled and skinned ⎦ Fry and grind

100 gms. charoli ⎤
100 gms. white pumpkin seeds
100 gms. red pumpkin seeds
100 gms. cucumber seeds
100 gms. melon seeds ⎬ Fry
400 gms. dried wheat milk
400 gms. dried water chestnuts ⎦

2 kgs. sugar
20 gms. cardamom & nutmeg powder
10 gms. mace powder
10 gms. piprimul-na-gathia powder
20 gms. dried ginger powder
10 gms. white pepper powder
10 gms. poppy seeds, fry
2 gms. pure kesar or saffron
300 ml. rose water
1600-1800 gms. pure ghee

- Make a strong syrup with the sugar and 10 cups of water. Bring to a roiling boil, remove from the fire, and allow to cool.

- Heat 500 gms. of pure ghee in an iron karahi or "kalai" vessel or any other strong vessel and fry the almonds, pistachios and charoli separately, and place in a large thali or tray. Fry the four white pumpkin, red pumpkin, cucumber and melon seeds separately, and place in the thali. Fry the water chestnuts and then the wheat milk separately. Add more ghee to the pan.

- Fry the poppy seeds lightly.

- Crush all the fried nuts and spices, the poppy seeds and grind fine.

- The saffron should be heated lightly on a skillet, crushed and mixed into the rose water.

- Whisk the egg yolks well. Mix in the remainder of the ghee and then add it to the sugar syrup and place the vessel on a medium flame and mix non-stop with a long handled chamach or perforated spoon, till you feel the mixture thickening. Add the ground nuts, the spices, the poppy seeds, the water chestnuts ground fine, the wheat milk ground fine and stir the mixture non-stop without letting up till the ghee separates and floats on top. Taste for sugar.

- Add the crushed saffron mixed in the rose water, mix well and remove the pan from the fire.

- Sprinkle the cardamom-nutmeg powder and the mace powder over the halwa and mix these aromatic spices well into it.

Preparation time	:	1 hour
Cooking time	:	1½ hours
Serves	:	25

- Pour into 2 greased aluminium square trays. Cool overnight. Next day, cut into the required pieces.
- Decorate with almond and pista slices.
- You will get about 6 kgs. eda paak.

BADAAM-PAAK

This is one of the easiest sweets to make. I have ground the almonds fine. But some people prefer them to be kept a little crunchy.

JAI VAKEEL'S BADAAM PAAK
AS GIVEN TO ME BY ROSHAN DALAL

2 gms. saffron
1 kg. almonds, boiled, skinned and
    ground – set
    some whole almonds aside for
    decoration
1 kg. mava, grated or mashed
1 kg. very high quality sugar
1 kg. pure ghee
600 ml. rose water (Chavi Chhap)

- Take a large kalai tapeli and put the sugar and rose water in it together and place on a very slow fire and when the syrup becomes thick, add the grated mava and mix non-stop till it has amalgamated well with the syrup. Then add the crushed almonds in small amounts and mix non-stop. Keep adding ghee a little at a time to help loosen up the mixture and continue to do so till all of it has been used up.
- Heat the saffron on an iron tava and then crumble it directly into the hot mixture. Keep stirring till the ghee separates from the mixture. This is a sign that it is ready. Remove from the fire and pour into glass dishes.
- Decorate the surface with the whole almonds.
- I would suggest using 150 gms. ghee less than given quantity.

Preparation time	:	1 hour
Cooking time	:	45 mins.
Serves	:	20

MEHERBAI WADIA-NI-KHARIA-NI-JELLY
(Meherbai Wadia's Trotters Jelly)

12 tender trotters, each cut into
   3 pieces
800 gms. sugar
3 sour limes for juice
1 tbsp. powdered nutmeg and
   cardamom
1 tsp. small pieces of cinnamon
½ tsp. crushed cloves
2 eggs
½ tsp. black tea leaves
2-3 tbsps. brandy (optional)
4-5 drops essence of rose or
   vanilla (optional)

- Clean the trotters well. Remove the bone between its hooves and wash 2 to 3 times.

- Place the trotters on a strong wooden board and hit the bones with a strong meat knife.

- Take a strong, thick bottomed kalai tapeli. Pour in 9 to 10 litres of water. Add the trotters to it. Place the tapeli on a medium flame and allow to cook the trotters till soft and only about 2 litres of water remains in the tapeli. Take a ladle and crush whatever jelly remains. Then place a sieve on top of a tapeli covered lightly with mulmul and pour all the soup through the sieve and cloth. Crush whatever remains through the cloth and squeeze out every drop of liquid you can. Cool the liquid.

- Tilt the tapeli a little, place some rags under it and carefully remove all the fat which has gathered on the surface of the liquid. You can do this with a soft piece of mulmul or a pierced chamach. No grease should be left on top of the liquid.

- Take an old soft piece of mulmul and pour the liquid through it onto a clean tapeli once again. I suggest you get someone to hold the mulmul whilst you pour the liquid.

- Place the sugar in a large clean tapeli and add the eggs – washed well. Then crush the eggs along with their shells into the sugar as well as you can.

- Add the trotter liquid to the sugar with the crushed eggs and mix the two vigorously for 5 minutes.

- Add the elchi-jaifal powder, the cinnamon pieces, the crushed cloves and the tea leaves and place the tapeli on a high flame. Keep stirring with a ladle till the liquid comes to a strong boil. Then change the flame to simmer.

- Then, pour the lime juice all around the tapeli and cover it with a lid. Remove the scum, if any, from the top of the liquid. Then put the ladle in the centre of the liquid. The liquid should be clear like glass. Remove from the fire.

- Pass this liquid once again through a mulmul cloth into a clean tapeli.

- You will now need a flannel bag. Overturn a 4 legged stool. Place a tapeli in its centre and tie the bag to the 4 legs of the stool with a thick string. Then pour the liquid into the bag, a little at a time, till it drips from the bag into the clean tapeli.

- On no account must you try to expedite the dripping process by shaking the bag or trying to mix the liquid with a spoon.

- After all the liquid has been passed through the flannel bag, pour some brandy into the liquid if you are going to use it. Allow the jelly to cool.

- You can add 4 to 5 drops of essence of rose or vanilla to the jelly when it is very cold.

- Pour into small, cocktail glasses and chill in the refrigerator.

NAVAJBAI FITTER-NI-KHARIA-NI-JELLY
(Navajbai Fitter's Recipe for Sheep's Trotters Jelly)

12 front leg sheep's trotters,
    each cut into 3 pieces
500 gms. sugar
3 egg whites
3-4 small cinnamon pieces
5 green cardamoms
4 cloves
1 tsp. tea leaves
3 sour limes, for juice
1 large tbsp. brandy (Optional)
2 kgs. ice

- Clean the bone between the sheep's hooves and wash them 2 to 3 times.

- Place the trotter pieces into a large tapeli and fully cover them with water. The water should be 2" above the trotters.

- Place the vessel on medium heat for at least 5 hours. You should keep adding more hot water to cook the trotters till tender. Then allow the water to evaporate till you have 4 large glassfuls of liquid left.

- Strain the liquid through a fine sieve into another tapeli. Cool it. Then remove the fat which has accumulated on top of the liquid. It should be completely removed.

- Add the sugar to the liquid, whisked egg whites, egg shells, and the cinnamon, cloves and cardamoms and replace on the fire and stir vigorously with a ladle.

- When the liquid has boiled for 5 minutes, add the juice of 3 sour limes and the tea leaves. After some time, you will see that the liquid jelly becomes very clear. Remove the scum with a perforated flat spoon or chamach.

- Strain the liquid through a piece of flannel. I strongly recommend Meherbai Wadia's use of a flannel bag tied to the 4 corners of an upturned stool.

- Allow the jelly to drip through and place it in a wet mould over ice. Mix in the brandy.

- In olden days, roughly 70 years ago when Navajbai Fitter lived, people did not have refrigerators. So they had to chill whatever they needed, on ice. We are lucky. All we have to do is place the mould into a refrigerator.

Preparation time	:	1 hour
Cooking time	:	5-6 hours
Serves	:	25

MUKTAD-NU-BHATIYU

Every year, during the last 10 days before Parsi Navroze or New Year, the Avestaic Hamaspathmaedeyo festival takes place. In Gujarati, we call this the "muktad days".

The Farvardin Yasht very clearly tells us that during these 10 days, the spirits of our dead departed come to visit us. When they see the prayers being performed in their memory, and the delicious food and brand new clothes laid out for them, they are very happy and bless the people who live in the house and who have gone to so much trouble for them. But if no one remembers them, they depart in tears and sadness.

So, our forefathers, living in the villages and cities of Gujarat would keep a room separate for these prayers. It was cleaned and washed and so were the 'behras' or silver vases and lotas belonging to all the deceased who were to be remembered. These vases, sometimes of crystal, were laid out on round or rectangular marble tables, having iron bases, painted white. Next to the table, a circular tripod stand, painted white, was placed to lay out the thala containing the food to be prayed over 3 times a day.

This was no joke for the women folk who had to slog night and day fetching wood and "handas" of water from wells. No servants could be used.

Next to the behras with the flowers, an 'afarganiu' of fire was kept along with a diva.

The 10-days 'muktad' start on Astad Roz in Spendarmad Mahino or month, and end on the last Gatha. The 18-days 'muktad' start on Ashishwang Roz and end on Amerdad Roz. The previous day is Khordad Saal, Zarathushtra's birthday. On this day, at night all the 'behras' are washed and turned over. This is called 'behra valaavi deva ni reet."

Now, on the first day of the 'muktad', i.e. on Astad Roz, the prayers are begun with 'Chai-nu-Satum' when the priest prays over a bowl of tea. On the first day, always, white maida puris and rava is kept in the thala. Various sweets are made every day, such as chapat, chaptis, bhakhras, karkarias, bhajias, kumas, aoondh, mysore paak, kopra paak, dal-ni-pori and khajur-ni-ghari. All these recipes can be found in my book, JAMVA CHALOJI No. 1.

This prayer is followed by baj which is held if in an Agiary or Atashbehram, within the pavis on hallowed ground. The afringan-farokshi is prayed in the hall set out for the 'muktads'. Here, the priest prays in front of a thali in which he places different fruits such as bananas, apples, oranges, mosambi, pomegranate, papaya, pineapple, melon, watermelon, grapes. Darun, unleavened flour cakes, crisp puris and malido accompany the fruit.

The third prayer is the "Bapor-nu-Satum', meaning lunch-time prayer. This contains regular food in the thali, such as rotlis, cutlets, fried fish, dar-chawal, etc.

Then there is a final 'satum' prayer, 'Sanj-nu-Satum' where, the priest prays before a night meal, consisting of vegetables, an egg dish and a mutton dish.

On the night of the last Gatha, the night before Hormazd Roz, which is our New Year or Navroze, prayers are recited at 2 a.m. Here, the prayer is called the 'Satum-nu-Afringan'. Baj is held and the 'Bhatiya-nu-Satum' is prayed by the Mobed. The Bhatiyu is like a picnic package, which the client takes home. This signifies the end of the 10 days' prayers.

The only Agiary in Bombay which still gives these "Bhatiyas" is the Mehella Patel Agiary, situated behind the Novelty Cinema in Grant Road. I personally went and met Allamai Katrak, the wife of the Panthaky, who manages the cooking of all the food set out in the Agiary. Once this brave lady is no more, I dread to think that the day of the Muktad-nu-Bhatiyu will be over.

Here is what goes into the makeup of the bhatiyu.

1. One complete half of a chicken-breast and leg called "antheli marghi'.

2. Guvarsing-ne-Gharab-no-Patio. The fish roe used has to be that of the Bhing Fish. The recipe is included in the book Jamva Chaloji No. 1.

3. An omelette made of eggs, adu-lasan, salt, pepper and a smidgeon of red chilli powder and fried in ghee.

4. Seven Bhakhras.

5. Two boiled eggs.

6. Finely chopped fried vegetables.

7. 2 Rotlis.

In olden days, in the villages, "daru" (liquor) and "tapkhir" or powdered tobacco, was also placed in the thali.

The last Gatha was also well-known for the whole community - men, women and children - reciting the "Patet Pashemani" prayer. It was recited at home or at the Agiary, wherever it was convenient. The community prayed for the atonements of any sins they had committed knowingly and unknowingly in thought, word or deed. This was our day of sorrow.

Non-Parsis, unfortunately, call our New Year, Pateti.

On New Year's day, many people celebrate with prayers for the dead. They place new clothes for the men and women in thalas and the priests pray over them. Even the poorest did so in days gone by. The sudreh and kusti were the most important part of these clothes that were set out.

Since the photograph for the "bhatiyu" was to be taken in the month of May, no bhing roe was available. I even telephoned Yazad Kolah in Navsari, but he said "No – no gharab". So we used fried "bois", mullets.

Rusi Katrak, a mobed at the Mehella Patel Agiary was gracious enough to arrange for the ceremony to be photographed and to be a part of the photograph.

ARDHA-CHAND
(Half Moons)

For the Pastry:

2 cups of self-raising flour
2 tbsps. pure ghee
A pinch of salt
Water

For the Maan:

1 cup ghee
Rice flour as required
Water

For the Mawa Stuffing:

2 cups of mawa
½ cup of finely boiled, skinned and
  chopped almonds
½ cup powdered sugar or to taste
Vanilla essence

**For the Rava and Dry-Fruit
Stuffing:**

1 cup semolina or rava
½ cup sugar or to taste
½ gm. saffron
1 tsp. poppy seeds or khuskhus,
  fried and lightly roasted
100 gms. boiled, skinned chopped
  pistachios
100 gms. boiled, skinned, chopped
  cashew nuts
50 gms. charoli
½ tsp. cardamom seeds

Preparation time	:	1 hour
Cooking time	:	45-50 mins.
Serves	:	6-10

- These pastry half moons were very popular items and were placed in all muktad preparations. They were stuffed with:
  - mawa and almond mixture
  - rava and dry fruit mixture
  - coconut-raisin and poppy seed mixture
  - chikkat ripe mango mixture

- The pastry was made with maida or self-raising flour as well as a mixture called "maan". This "maan" consisted of whipped ghee and rice flour. The ghee was creamed by hand, and then rice flour was added to it little by little, until it became a light buttery mass which could be held in the hand. This mass was placed in ice and ice-cold water to become firm. Then, it was used the next day. Creaming the ghee takes the stuffing out of one.

- Place the self-raising flour, salt and 2 tablespoons of ghee in a thali and knead the two until you get a crumbled mixture. Add a little water at a time and knead well until you get a soft, supple dough. Cover with a damp cloth and ready your stuffing.

- Divide the kneaded flour dough into 4 balls. Roll out 1 ball at a time into a huge rotli. Take a lump of the "maan" in your right hand and apply it carefully over the rolled dough, leaving a ¼" of space free within the edge of the rotli. Sprinkle a little rice flour on top of the "maan". Then, carefully, using both your hands, double the big rotli into a half moon. Apply some "maan" on the dough, sprinkle a little rice flour and double it up into the shape of a quarter circle. Then roll up into a rotli again. Do the same with the other rotlis. Take a small ball from one of these rotlis and roll into a small puri shape, on a wooden board.

For the Coconut-Raisin-Poppy Seed Stuffing:

½ cup grated fresh coconut
¾ cup sugar
1 tsp. nutmeg-cardamom powder
½ cup washed and dried raisins

For the Chikkat Mango Stuffing:

4 Alphonso mangoes, peeled and cut
½ cup sugar
¼ tsp. green cardamom seeds

- Place as much stuffing as you can on half the side of the puri. Then apply water or (flour and water cooked together) chikki, ½" around the edges of the puri. Fold the empty ½ over the stuffed half and press the semi-circle of the puri with pressure, so that, both the sides stick together. Then pick up the half moon and pinch the sides together between your thumb and finger, to give the edge a ropy effect.

- Make as many stuffed half moons as you can. The numbers depend upon the size of your puris and the amount of stuffing you use.

- Place a karahi, half filled with ghee on a medium flame. Use vegetable ghee, such as Dalda, if pure is not available. When the ghee gets hot, lower the flame, and fry the half moons in small batches stirring them all the time you are frying, so that they do not stick to each other or get a dark colour. Fry till very lightly golden or a deep ivory colour and remove from the heat and allow to cool.

- **Cooking The Stuffings: Mawa Stuffing**
  Grate and mash the mawa until it is smooth. Knead it a little so no clots exist and then put it in a heavy-bottomed kalai patia or langri. Place over a very low fire and mix the mawa from side to side until it becomes soft and oozes a little grease. Then sprinkle it with the finely chopped almonds and the powdered sugar and spices. Mix it all well until the sugar becomes one with the mawa. Remove from the fire and cool. Stuff it into the puris as described above. Pleat the sides between two fingers and when ready, fry in hot ghee.

- **Rava and Dryfruit Stuffing:**
  Take 1 cup rawa and 1 tablespoon ghee and roast the rava lightly over an iron skillet with a very heavy bottom, over a very low fire. Add the saffron. Keep mixing it up and down with a wad of muslin. Keep the rawa white. It should not be allowed to brown. Roast it for about 5 minutes and add the 3 types of nuts and the roasted poppy

seeds and the sugar and mix and roast until the sugar liquidizes. Remove from the fire and cool. Then fill the puris and fry as described above.

- **Coconut-Raisin Stuffing:**
  Place the coconut, sugar and a ¼ cup water into a heavy-based kalai langri. Place over a low fire and allow the sugar to melt and cook till the coconut has cooked and absorbed the sugar syrup. Add the washed, dried raisins and cook for 3 minutes more. Remove from the fire when the coconut mixture has become tight. Sprinkle the nutmeg-cardamom powder, mix well and cool. Stuff the puris and fry as described above.

- **Chikkat Mango Stuffing:**
  Place the sugar and cardamom seeds along with ¾ cup water in a small vessel and boil it till it become sticky. Add the mango pieces, lower the flame and stir gently, until the syrup has dried up. Then stuff the puris and pinch the sides in a rope design.

PAKKI-KERI-MA-GOS

(Mutton Cooked with Ripe Mangoes)

1 tbsp. ginger-garlic paste
750 gms. mutton chunks with nali, washed
6 large ripe mangoes, any type
3 large onions, finely chopped
1½ tsps. red chilli powder
1 tbsp. garam masala
½ tsp. shahjeera powder
½ tsp. mace powder
½ tsp. caraway seeds
3 whole Kashmiri chillies, deseeded
1 gm saffron
Salt
Pure ghee

- Apply salt and ginger-garlic paste to the washed mutton and place in a cool spot for ½ hour.

- Take a langri and place 3 tablespoons of ghee in it. Add the finely chopped onion and cook over a medium heat till the onions are a pale brown. Then lower the heat, add the mutton and cover it and cook it for 7 minutes in its own juice. Then sprinkle the chilli powder, garam masala, shahjeera and mace powders over the mutton and mix well and stir for 3 more minutes, keeping the flame low.

- Put the mutton in a pressure cooker with sufficient water and cook till it is soft and tender.

- Whilst the mutton is cooking, skin the mangoes. Cut the flesh from the 2 cheeks of each mango into 4 pieces. You will get 8 pieces per mango. That is 48 pieces. Cut the sides so you get 2 pieces from each side. That will be 4 long pieces from each mango. So from 6 mangoes, you get 24 side pieces.

- Once the mutton is cooked, taste for salt and empty it into a clean langri or patia. Set it on the fire over a low flame and put the mangoes on top of the mutton. Coarsely crush the caraway seeds and sprinkle over the mango pieces. Allow to simmer for 12 to 15 minutes until the mango pieces have mixed with the mutton gravy and have become very soft.

- Place the saffron on an iron tava and make it crisp. Then put it in ¼ cup of hot water and squeeze the strands till the water becomes yellow and pour it over the mango and mutton pieces. Mix gently and simmer for 5 minutes more. Then remove from the fire.

- Serve with hot rotlis and a kachumber made from spring onions.

Preparation time	:	10 mins.
Cooking time	:	45 mins.
Serves	:	6-8

ALLAMAI KATRAK-NI-PAKKI-KERI-GOS-MA

(Allamai Katrak's Ripe Mangoes Cooked with Mutton)

500 gms. mutton chunks with nali,
  washed twice
7 ripe Alphonso mangoes, skinned,
  kept whole
1 large onion, finely chopped
400 gms. small onions, cut vertically
  into half and each half cut into
  3 long pieces
1 tbsp. ground ginger-garlic paste
1½ tsp. red chilli powder
1 tbsp. cumin, coarsely ground
1 tbsp. Allamai Katrak's dhana-jeera
  masala
Salt
Ghee

Preparation time	:	12 mins.
Cooking time	:	35-40 mins.
Serves	:	4-6

- Marinade the mutton in salt and ginger-garlic paste

- Place the large onion in 3 tablespoons of ghee in a broad tapeli over a medium flame. Cook till it browns and then add the cumin, chilli powder and dhana-jeera masala. Lower the flame, cook the masala till red and add the mutton and allow to cook for 7 minutes. Add the rest of the chopped onions and cover and cook till it browns.

- Place the mutton along with the gravy into a pressure cooker. Mix in the skinned mangoes gently. Add sufficient water so that the mutton turns tender.

- Taste for salt and serve hot with parathas and a hot chilli pickle.

Allamai Katrak's Ripe Mangoes
with Mutton (1)
Roasted whole Chicken (2)
Dried Bombay Duck Patia with
Red Pumpkin and
Banana & Slices (3)

TADI-NO-BATERVO

(Mutton Cooked in Toddy)

This fantastic dish was cooked in a large terrocotta "ghariya" or pot. Don't worry. Use a "kalai" tapeli or any heavy bottomed high sided vessel.

2 kgs. top quality mutton leg from a male goat, cut into 2" chunks
7 bottles toddy – should be on the sweeter side
10 green chillies, slit and deseeded
1 bunch fresh coriander, finely chopped
½ bunch fresh mint leaves only
75 gms. fresh ginger
75 gms. garlic, large cloves
1½ tsps. turmeric powder
15 fresh black peppercorns, coarsely grounded
7 cloves
1½ tbsps. Parsi dhansakh masala
Coarse salt

Preparation time	:	20 mins.
Cooking time	:	1½ to 2 Hr.
Serves	:	10-12

• Wash the mutton pieces well. Lightly crack the nali bones so its easy to get access to the marrow. Marinade in salt.

• Grind the coriander, mint, green chillies, ginger, garlic and all the spices till soft and fine and apply it to the mutton pieces. Then place them in the vessel in which you are going to cook it. Allow to marinade for 2 hours.

• Pour 3 bottles of toddy into the vessel with the mutton, cover tightly and place on medium heat. After the toddy mixture has boiled for about 30 minutes, lower the flame, add 2 more bottles of toddy and cook for 2 hours till over half the liquid has evaporated. The meat should feel tender and the gravy sticky with the mutton marrow and fat.

• Serve with rice rotlis or white ghee rice, a green tomato and beetroot salad and mango chutney.

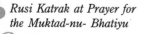

Rusi Katrak at Prayer for the Muktad-nu- Bhatiyu

TADI-MA-SEKTA-NI-SING
(Drumsticks Cooked in Toddy)

6 large tender drumsticks, each stringed and cut into 3" pieces

½ grated coconut
4 green chillies, deseeded
1 bunch fresh coriander, chopped fine
8 large cloves garlic, chopped fine
1 ½" ginger, chopped fine
1 tsp. (cut) turmeric powder
1 tsp. (cut) black pepper powder
} Grind together

¾ bottle strong pure toddy
2 sprigs curry leaves
Salt
Pure Ghee

Preparation time	:	7-10 mins.
Cooking time	:	15 mins.
Serves	:	6

- If you like, tie the drumsticks into little bundles of 4 pieces each. If not, leave the pieces loose.

- Place 3 tablespoons of ghee in a large pan. Formerly, my great grandmother would do most of her cooking in huge carinated terracotta bowls called "peni". Heat the ghee and drop in the ground masala and the curry sprigs and mix and stir till you get a delicious whiff. Then, put in the drumsticks, toddy and salt and cook over a high fire and cook till the drumsticks are tender.

- Serve hot with ghee rice, papads and pani-nu-keri-nu-achaar.

GARAM-SEKELI-TADI
(Hot Toddy)

About 2 bottles sweet-sour toddy in a terracotta toddy container called "ghariyu"
6 large garlic cloves, skinned and lightly crushed between your palms
1 tsp. freshly grounded black peppercorns
Salt to taste, if desired

Preparation time	:	8 mins.
Cooking time	:	15-20 mins.
Serves	:	4-6

- Place the "ghariyu" with the toddy, garlic and black pepper powder on the fire and warm it. Do not boil the toddy.

- Just in case your toddy has turned sour, add a lemon sized ball of jaggery.

- Pour the warm toddy in glasses and serve straight from the "ghariyu".

Sweets

TEA-TIME TREATS AND MUKTAD SWEETS

In the villages of Gujarat, there were no bakeries until the last couple of decades. When we went to "gaam" in May every year, we took along stacks of French Toast and ladis of bread for the uncles and great-grandmother and great-grandfather. Coconuts were rare. My great-grandfather did not have a single tree on his land. Those who had them were considered very lucky. So, amongst our luggage, would be coconuts, fresh ginger, tea and packets of Belapur sugar, which my father would buy as gifts.

The coconuts were sparingly used. At least, one was used to make fish curry but the rest were kept for sweet making.

A very simple, delicious, rare tea treat was hot wheat flour rotlis stuffed with a sweet coconut mixture made with jaggery and rose water. Half moon wheat flour crescents were made with grated coconut and raisins cooked in sugar syrup. One strange item was, rice flour rotlis stuffed with sweet mawa.

Another very nice tea time sweet was wheat flour rose flavoured squares, deep fried in ghee and dipped in a hot pink sugar syrup and removed quickly and served cold.

Very rarely, in May, the abovementioned floured squares were stuffed with a mixture of ripe crimson, mango growing in front of Soonamai's cottage.

Savoury treats consisted of rotlis and puris stuffed with thick, dry masala toovar dal, or raw, sour mango mixtures spiced up with chillies.

One of the most popular tea time items, were fresh potato chips, slathered with sour cream mixed with green chillies and coriander. Sometimes, the potato chips were coated with crushed broiled sesame seeds and dried red chillies.

Very often bhajias were made. They were very different from those we eat in hotels, clubs and gymkhanas these days. Whatever vegetable was at hand, was brought into use.

Red pumpkin was skinned and sliced into rectangles and marinated in vinegar, sugar and spices and then fried in a batter of gram flour. Prawns were often fried in a thick and hot flour and egg batter – we never got to eat them as the uncles ate them up with their hot drinks. Tiny baby golden fish were also fried to a crisp and had as snacks.

Dairy products were used to the maximum as it meant a saving of money. Many milk based, mava based and cream based items were used for sweets, snacks and for meal times.

The month of May was the worst in the Gujarat villages of old. The farms had to rely solely on what they cultivated themselves and the land burnt with heat and turned dry.

Nowadays, we are used to trucks bringing us fruits and vegetables across India. In the olden days, it was not so. Every type of vegetable which could be dehydrated on the rooftops, was cleaned, collected and stored in large glass and terracotta jars.

CHAWAL-NA-AATA-NI-KHEER
(Rice Flour Dessert)

Soonamai had a huge grinding stone on her back verandah. Actually it was two huge round stones set up on a wooden stand. There was a large hole in the stone on top to trickle the wheat or rice and a wooden handle, also set in the top stone. Two female servants would squat next to it with their legs spread out and grind the daily quota of rice for the rotlis. One stack of rotlis was needed at breakfast time and a larger one was made for the night meal. Fifty to sixty years ago, people ground their own rice and wheat as there were no electric chakkis to do the job.

As a young child I would shout and skip around and demand to be allowed to help in the grinding, but it was hard work pushing the heavy stones round and round with the right hand and feeding the grains into the mouth with the left hand. This was called "patthar-ni-ghanti".

The rice was threshed on the wide verandah on the side of the house. Round wooden cups, double the size of our teacups were embedded into the verandah floor. Then, heavy circular, wooden poles, made smooth with years of use were brought out. The end of the heavy poles had metal bases. These were called "musarus'. The floor was freshly cleaned and an application of cow dung was applied to the floor, and allowed to dry for 2 days.

Every large family had its own "ghantis" and "musarus".

The freshly ground flour made rotlis, parathas and desserts taste extra delicious.

Today, all we have to do is go to the market and buy packets of wheat flour, self-raising flour, arrow root and cornflour.

I suggest that rice flour should always be ground fresh in the mixer-grinder at home.

Many people do not directly grind rice if using it for desserts. They wash the rice and spread it out in the sun on a white sheet to dry. When crisp, it is ground and used for cakes, puddings, crepes and rolls.

CHOKHA-NE-GULAB-NI-KHEER

(Rice & Rose Kheer)

100 gms. broken rice
2 litres creamy milk
2 cups sugar
2 tsps. rose essence
½ tsp. cochineal red colour
2 pink petalled roses

Preparation time	:	Nil
Cooking time	:	35 mins.
Serves	:	4-6

- Crush the rice and cook it in a pressure cooker with 2 cups of water till soft.

- Place the cooked rice in a large patia along with the milk and sugar over a low heat and keep mixing it for 15 minutes on simmer. By this time, a lot of water will have evaporated and the rice should have blended well with the milk and become a sweet, sticky mixture.

- Remove from the stove and mix in the rose essence and cochineal. Place in a glass bowl. Chill overnight and serve decorated with pink rose petals.

SERDI-NE-CHAVAL-NI-KHEER

(Sugarcane Juice and Rice Kheer)

This was a very good method of using up leftover cooked rice in the olden days.

10 cups sugarcane juice
2 cups boiled cooked rice
1½ tsps. cardamom powder

Preparation time	:	5 mins.
Cooking time	:	35-40 mins.
Serves	:	8-10

- Place the juice in a large tapeli and cook over a medium flame until the juice is reduced to almost half its quantity.

- Mash the boiled rice on a stone queen or a mixer-grinder with a little water. Then add it to the boiling juice and keep stirring on and off until it begins to thicken. Add the cardamom powder, stir and take it off the fire.

- Serve hot or cold in individual bowls.

CHOKHA-NA-AATA-NI-KHEER
(Rice Flour Sweet)

150 gms. rice flour
250 gms. sugar
1 litre milk
20 gms. almond, boiled, skinned, sliced
20 gms. seedless raisins
4 tsps. rose water
4 green cardamom seeds only, crushed
Pure ghee

Preparation time	:	Nil
Cooking time	:	30-40 mins.
Serves	:	8

- Take a heavy bottomed kalai langri. Place the rice flour in it and add 1¼ litre water and stir both together to make a smooth mixture.

- Gently fry the almond slices and raisins in pure ghee and set aside.

- Place the mixed rice flour and water on a medium flame. Stir non-stop till it thickens. This should take at least 10 minutes. Once the mixture is thick, add the milk and the sugar and stir vigorously till there are no granules in the liquid and it has become smooth. Keep stirring till you feel it thickening and becoming firm. Taste for sugar and remove from the fire and add the cardamom seeds and rose water and mix again.

- Ladle the kheer onto a flat bottomed glass dish and sprinkle with the fried almond slices and raisins.

GULABI-KHEER-BADAM-SAATHE
(Pink Almond Kheer)

100 gms. rice flour
1 litre milk
1 cup sugar
150 gms. almonds, boiled, skinned, minced
½ cup rose sherbet or to taste

Preparation time	:	15 mins.
Cooking time	:	15 mins.
Serves	:	4-6

- Place the milk and sugar in a saucepan. Mix the rice flour till smooth in ½ to ¾ cup of water. Add to the milk.

- Place the saucepan over a low flame and keep stirring non-stop until the mixture boils and begins to thicken. Add the minced almonds. Allow to thicken as much as possible. Remove from the fire and cool.

- Add the rose sherbet to the cooled kheer. Whisk well and distribute the mixture between crystal bowls or fancy glasses on stand. Chill overnight. Cover each bowl with foil.

- Serve the next day decorated with the blanched almonds.

PISTA-NI-KHEER
(Pistachio Kheer)

1 litre milk
150 gms. boiled, skinned, chopped, pistachios
1 cup sugar
6 drops green food colouring
½ cup rice flour
Pista flakes for decoration

Preparation time	:	10 mins.
Cooking time	:	40 mins.
Serves	:	6-8

- Heat the milk and sugar in a large patia. When the milk boils, add the pistas and keep boiling for 20 minutes, till the milk reduces in quantity.

- Mix the rice flour in ½ cup of water and add it to the boiling milk and stir non-stop till the milk thickens to a porridge like consistency. Remove from the fire and cool.

- Add the green food drops to the cold kheer and whisk well. Divide the kheer between 6 to 8 crystal bowls.

- Serve thoroughly chilled, decorated with pista flakes.

SEV-NI-KHEER
(Vermicelli Cooked in Milk)

200 gms. vermicelli
1¼ litre milk
1 cup sugar
50 gms. seedless raisins
50 gms. almond, boiled, skinned and sliced
1 tsp. cardamom-nutmeg powder
4 tsps. rose water
Pure ghee

Preparation time	:	Nil
Cooking time	:	20-25 mins.
Serves	:	6

- Place the broken vermicelli pieces along with 6 teaspoons of pure ghee and ½ litre of water in a kalai langri over a low flame. Gently mix and cover the vessel and cook until all the water has evaporated. Do not allow the sev to mash.

- Add the milk and sugar to the boiled vermicelli and cook on a medium flame till the mixture boils. Allow to simmer for 10 minutes and remove from the fire. Mix in the cardamom-nutmeg powder and the rose water.

- Pour the cooked vermicelli into a glass bowl or several small silver bowls.

- Fry the almond slices and raisins and top the vermicelli with them.

- Chill before eating.

RAVA-NI-KHEER
(Semolina Sweet)

150 gms. rava
1 litre creamy milk
275 gms. sugar
2 tbsps. fried sliced almonds
2 tbsps. fried seedless raisins
1 tsp. coarsely ground cardamom
    seeds
3 tsps. rose water
Pure ghee

Preparation time	:	Nil
Cooking time	:	20-25 mins.
Serves	:	6

- Place the rava and about ½ litre water in a kalai patia. Place on medium heat and stir till the rava is thick and cooked. Then add the sugar and milk and place over a low flame and keep stirring on simmer for 15 to 20 more minutes till the rava is smooth and moves like cream. Add 1 tablespoon pure ghee and remove from the fire.

- Mix the rose water and cardamom seeds into the hot rava.

- Ladle it onto a glass bowl and top with the fried sliced almonds and raisins.

SABUDANA-NI-KHEER
(Sago Sweet)

150 gms. sago
1 litre milk
300 gms. sugar
1 tsp. cardamom-nutmeg powder
3 tsps. rose water

Preparation time	:	Nil
Cooking time	:	30 mins.
Serves	:	6

- Clean the sago for any tiny stones and soak in ¾ litres of water in a kalai langri. Place on a medium flame and keep stirring till the sago is cooked and the mixture thickens and becomes sticky.

- Add the sugar and milk and lower the flame. Stir the mixture and allow it to boil till it becomes thick. Remove from the fire.

- Stir in the cardamom-nutmeg powder and the rose water and fill small katoris with the sago. Chill and serve.

HOMAI NALLADARU'S MAWA-NO-KOPRA-PAAK
(Homai Nalladaru's Coconut Barfi with Mawa)

3 coconuts, freshly grated
1 kg. sugar
2 litres milk
100 gms. sliced, fried almonds
　　(reserve some slices for
　　decoration)
100 gms. broken cashew nuts
2 tsps. crushed cardamom seeds
1½ tsps. icecream essence
2 tsps. pure ghee

Preparation time	:	15 mins.
Cooking time	:	30 mins.
Serves	:	15-20

- Place the grated coconuts in a large patia.

- Warm the milk and add it to the coconut. Mix in the sugar.

- Put the patia on a low fire and stir non-stop until it slowly thickens and becomes dry. Add ghee, essence and crushed cardamom seeds. Mix for 3 more minutes and cool. Cover with fried almond slices.

- Pour into a fancy rectangular dish or 2 circular dishes. Refrigerate.

- Cut into pieces the next day.

KERI-NI-BARFI
(Mango Barfi)

2 cups mawa
1 cup milk
1 cup sugar
2 cups mango pulp
20 gms. sliced pistachios

- Grate the mawa and place it in a heavy kalai patia. Add milk and stir over a very slow fire till the mawa gets melted in the milk. Keep stirring so that the mixture does not stick to the bottom. Add the sugar and keep stirring until you get a thick liquid resembling condensed milk.

- Add the fruit pulp and stir vigorously until the pulp has mixed totally with the thickened milk. Stir until the mixture thickens and can no longer be stirred in a circular motion. Remove from the stove and pour into a greased glass or silver container. Flatten the top and sprinkle liberally with the sliced pistachios.

- Allow to remain in a cool place for 6 hours or overnight before cutting it into pieces.

Preparation time	:	Nil
Cooking time	:	25 mins.
Serves	:	8-10

KHAND VAI
(Rice Flour Sweet)

400 gms. sugar
1 litre milk
Milk of 1 coconut } Mix
400 gms. rice flour
20 gms. almonds, boiled, skinned and sliced & fried
20 gms. pistachios, boiled, skinned, sliced & fried
2 tsps. cardamom-nutmeg powder
4 tsps. rose water
Pure ghee

Preparation time	:	Nil
Cooking time	:	30-35 mins
Serves	:	8

- Place the flour in a heavy-bottomed langri and add 5 tablespoons ghee and roast the flour over a low heat till it is ivory coloured.

- Add half a litre of water and mix the flour smoothly in it.

- Then add the milk, coconut milk and sugar and stir vigorously. There should be no lumps. Taste for sugar.

- Place the vessel over a low fire and keep stirring with a long handled chamach till the liquid starts getting thicker and thicker and it becomes difficult to stir it. This will take at least 25 minutes. Remove from the fire and add the cardamom-nutmeg powder and the rose water and stir once more.

- Take a greased aluminium tray and ladle the mixture into it and smoothen and level the surface with a spatula. Sprinkle the almond slivers and raisins over the surface. Cool.

- Cut into pieces the next day. Use for *chai-nu-loban* on muktad days.

KESRI PENDA
(Saffron Pedas)

This is one of the easiest desserts to make and keeps well for several days if kept in an airtight tin or a refrigerator. Hence, it was the housewives' favourite sweet and was especially made in advance so that the pendas could be used for the muktad "chai-nu-loban" which had to have a sweet in it. The kesri pendas became yellow in colour. If you make them without saffron, they still look good. Cardamom seeds are used instead.

Farming communities in Gujarat had no problems as regards dairy products. All their surplus milk was turned into curds from which butter was made in huge wooden containers swung between poles. One or two female servants would churn the curds into butter which was made into ghee. The chaas or buttermilk was enjoyed by the family and the surplus was given to the servants to take home.

Malai, paneer, sweet curds, mawa and milk was used in profusion. It was only the very poor villagers, who had no cows, who had to buy milk. The town and city dwellers bought all their milk items. Until 40 years ago, topli paneer and malai, were sent each evening by train from Surat, direct to the rich sethias' houses in Bombay city.

All in all, the wealthier farmers lived a life of great ease and plenty.

One very easy way to make pendas was to take one litre milk and add crisp saffron to it and boil it and boil it until a soft mawa was formed. It was then mixed with ½ to ¾ cups of powdered sugar until the mawa and sugar were one. Then ½ tsp. of pure ghee was used to grease both the hands. Small balls of the mixture were made and then flattened from top and allowed to cool. These were stored in airtight containers and used within a week. Nowadays, most of the pendas are made from commercially available mawas bought from milk shops.

To 1 kilo mawa, add ¾ cup of powdered sugar. The mawa is first heated over a low fire and stirred back and forth until it became soft. Cool the mawa and mix in the sugar and roll into a ball. Small round balls of this mixture are made, slightly flattened on the top, and studded with raisins or cardamom seeds or sliced almonds.

Preparation time	:	15 mins.
Cooking time	:	45-50 mins.
Serves	:	6-10

KESARIYA BARFI
(Saffron Barfi)

2 gms. saffron
2 cups of mawa, grated
1 cup of milk
1 cup of sugar
½ cup crushed, boiled, skinned
    almonds, lightly toasted
10 cardamom seeds

Preparation time	:	Nil
Cooking time	:	30-35 mins.
Serves	:	6-8

- Place the grated mawa and the milk in a heavy bottomed pan over a very slow fire and keep stirring round and round till the mawa melts and becomes one with the milk and you get a thick liquid without any lumps. Heat the saffron on an iron tava and crush it into the milk.

- Add the sugar and keep stirring until the liquid becomes sticky. If one drop placed in a saucer of water becomes firm and steady, the milk is ready. Remove from the fire and add the cardamom seeds and crushed almonds. Stir vigorously and pour into a greased glass or silver dish.

- Flatten the dish and sprinkle the sliced almonds on top of the barfi. Keep overnight in a cool place, before cutting it into pieces.

ALOO VAZIR-NO-CHIKOO-NO-HALWO

(Aloo Vazir's Chikoo Halwa)

12 large ripe chikoos
500 gms. mawa
2 cups sugar
1 tin condensed milk
1 tsp. vanilla essence
50 gms. butter
50 gms. almonds
50 gms. pistachios
50 gms. cashew nuts
20 gms. raisins

Preparation time	:	10 mins.
Cooking time	:	30 mins.
Serves	:	25 pieces

- Skin the chikoos, cut into 4, remove the seeds and the white pith.

- Place the sugar in a heavy bottomed pan and add the skinned chikoos and crush them to a pulp by hand. Place on a low fire and allow to cook till the sugar melts and slowly starts to thicken. Add the condensed milk and butter and mix thoroughly till it becomes hot.

- Divide the nuts and raisins into 2 parts. Crush one portion coarsely and add to the chikoo. Slice the other portion and use to decorate the halwa.

- Heat the mava in a clean vessel and when soft, add to the chikoo pulp and cook till well blended over a low fire.

- Grease a glass or silver dish and spread the chikoo halwa into it. Decorate with the sliced nuts and raisins.

ALOO VAZIR-NO-SAPARCHAN-NO-HALWO

(Aloo Vazir's Apple Halwa)

500 gms. apples, skinned, cored
  and grated
250 gms. mawa
1 tin condensed milk
2 cups sugar
1 tsp. pineapple essence
50 gms. almonds
50 gms. pistachios
50 gms. cashew nuts
20 gms. seedless raisins
50 gms. butter

Preparation time	:	10 mins.
Cooking time	:	30 mins.
Serves	:	25 pieces

• Take a heavy bottomed vessel. Place the apples in the tapeli along with the sugar on a low fire and allow the sugar to melt. Keep stirring till the apples are totally mashed.

• When the sugar has melted, add the condensed milk and 50 grams of butter and keep stirring over a low flame till all the ingredients have been well blended. Cool.

• Divide the almond, pistachios, cashew nuts and raisins into 2 parts. Put half the amount coarsely crushed, in the apple and sugar mixture and allow to simmer on a slow heat for 3 to 4 minutes more.

• Heat the mawa over a low fire in a clean vessel till soft. Cool and mix into the apple.

• Grease a glass dish and empty out the mixture onto it.

• Decorate with the remainder of the sliced almonds, pistachios, cashew nuts and raisins.

Kesar Penda (1)
Sada Penda (2)
Pista Barfi (3)
Aloo Vazir's Chickoo Barfi (4)
Mango Barfi (5)

SAPARCHAN-NI-JALEBI

(Apple Jalebis)

4 large round red or golden apples – they should be firm

For the Batter:

2 eggs, whisked
1 cup self-raising flour
½ cup cream
1½ cups milk
5 tbsps castor sugar
1 tsp. vanilla essence
1 tsp. cardamom-nutmeg powder
Breadcrumbs
Ghee (Dalda or pure)

- Take a deep glass bowl. Put in the self-raising flour, sugar, vanilla and spice powder and mix lightly. Then, gradually stir in the milk and mix in circles until the batter is smooth. Whisk the cream lightly and stir it into the batter along with the whisked eggs. Allow the batter to settle for 2 hours.

- Just before it is needed, heat a karahi half filled with ghee or dalda. When the ghee becomes hot, lower the heat a little and try one jalebi out to see how the batter coats the apple slice.

- Whilst the ghee is heating, peel the apples and slice them. The slices should be at least ¼" thick. Remove the center core carefully.

- Dip one slice into the batter and then pop it into the hot oil. If the batter sticks to the apple slice, it will turn a golden brown and swell up and cook in 2 minutes. Remove from the hot ghee and fry the other slices the same way.

- If for some reason the batter does not adhere to the apple, roll the slices in the breadcrumbs, dip into the batter, and fry till golden brown.

- Serve hot with dudh pak, basoondi or vanilla ice cream.

Preparation time	:	17 mins.
Cooking time	:	20-25 mins.
Serves	:	6-8

Green Sticky Almond Halwa (1)
Cooked Vermicelli (2)
Gulab Jamuns (3)

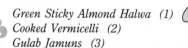

KATY DALAL-NO-SAPARCHAN-NO-HALWO

(Katy Dalal's Apple Sweet)

300 gms. mawa
500 gms. apples, skinned, cored,
  cut fine or grated
250 ml. (1 cup) milk
300 gms. sugar
6 cardamom seeds only
20 gms. boiled, sliced, fried almonds

Preparation time	:	15 mins.
Cooking time	:	30-40 mins.
Serves	:	8

- Heat sugar and apples in 1 cup milk till the sugar melts and most of the water dried up. Heat the mawa over a slow flame.

- Add the hot softened mawa to the apple and mix round and round. Add the cardamom seeds and cook mixture over a slow fire till sticky. The apple halwa will be an aromatic ivory coloured sweet. Taste for sugar.

- Pour into a clean glass or stainless steel vessel. Allow to cool overnight.

- For decoration, sprinkle with sliced, fried almonds. Cut into squares.

MALAI-NO-HALWO

(Cream Halwa)

1½ gms. saffron
750 gms. sugar
500 gms. malai or fresh cream
200 gms. mawa, grated
150 gms. almonds, boiled, skinned,
  sliced
150 gms. pistachios, boiled, skinned,
  sliced
100 gms. charoli, fried lightly
1 tbsp. suji or rava
½ cup rose water
½ tsp. nutmeg-cardamom powder
200 gms. or more pure ghee

Preparation time	:	20 mins.
Cooking time	:	35 mins.
Serves	:	7

- Place the cream and ghee in a large langri. Place it on low heat, stir for 5 minutes and add the rava. After you have stirred for 5 more minutes, add the grated mawa, stir for 3 to 4 minutes and take the vessel off the heat.

- Place the sugar and rose water into a deep tapeli. Mix well and place on a very low heat stirring all the time till it becomes thick and tight. Add the cream mixture and stir non-stop.

- Heat the saffron on an iron tava, make it crisp and add to the malai and sugar mixture. Stir rapidly for 3 minutes till the saffron has mixed well. Then add the almonds, pistachios, charoli and nutmeg-cardamom powder. Stir for 5 minutes and remove the vessel from the heat.

- Pour into a greased thali or aluminium tray and level the surface with a spatula. Cool overnight. Next day, cut into desired size pieces.

SAFED-KOHRA-NO-HALWO

(Ash Gourd Halwa)

2 kg. white gourd with skin, pith and seeds removed and grated
3 litres full cream milk
Sugar, weight of the gourd
200 gms. pistachios, boiled, skinned, sliced and fried
½ tsp. green colour
1 tsp. rose essence
3 tbsps. pure ghee

- Squeeze the grated gourd until all the water has run out. Collect the water in a tapeli. Weigh the grated, squeezed, gourd.

- Place the squeezed gourd into a heavy-based tapeli and cook till almost soft in 4 cups of its own water. Cook over a low fire so that the liquid does not evaporate very fast. When it has almost dried up, pour in the milk. Now the heavy, uphill work begins.

- Keep stirring the gourd mixture on a medium flame non-stop. When half the milk has evaporated, add the cardamom seeds. If you get tired of stirring the mixture, alternate with someone else.

- Add as much sugar as the weight of the grated gourd, and stir vigorously till the milk and sugar begin to dry up and you are left with a thick porridge-like consistency.

- Add half the sliced pistachios and the ghee and stir for 5 minutes and remove from the fire.

- Add the green colour and the rose essence and mix well till the halwa has changed into a light green colour.

- Pour into glass dishes and decorate with the remaining sliced nuts.

- Serve hot or cold.

Preparation time	:	30 mins.
Cooking time	:	1 hour or more
Serves	:	20

BADAM-NO-DAMIDO
(Almond Sweet)

500 gms. sugar
350 gms. almonds, ground
350 gms. mawa
175 gms. rawa or semolina
1 gm. kesar or saffron
½ tsp. ground nutmeg-cardamom
   powder
125 gms. ghee

Preparation time	:	20 mins.
Cooking time	:	30-40 mins.
Serves	:	6-8

- Place the sugar in a heavy-bottomed kalai patia along with 2 cups of water. Place on a medium heat and make a strong, thick syrup. A drop put into a saucer of water should congeal immediately. Remove from the fire.

- Grind the almonds.

- Place the rawa and ghee into a clean large tapeli and place over a medium heat and roast the rawa. Add the ground almonds, the mawa, the nutmeg-cardamom powder and the thick syrup and mix vigorously non-stop.

- Heat the saffron over an iron tava till crisp. Sprinkle it, by crushing with your fingers into the syrup mixture.

- Keep mixing the rawa, mawa and syrup until it all becomes one mass.

- Place it into a greased tray and level it with a spatula and allow to cool.

- Cut into diamond shapes.

LEELO-BADAM-NO-CHIKKAT-HALWO
(Green Sticky Almond Halwa)

300 gms. ghehu-nu-dudh (wheat milk)
800 gms. sugar
12 whole almonds, skinned, boiled, for decoration
20 whole pistachios, boiled, for decoration
250 gms. almonds, skinned, boiled and cut horizontally
2 sour limes for juice
¼ tsp. green food colour
4 green cardamom seeds only
1 tsp. vanilla essence
450-500 gms. pure ghee

Preparation time	:	20 mins.
Cooking time	:	1 Hour
Serves	:	10

- Soak the wheat milk in 2 cups of water.

- Place the sugar in a heavy bottomed langri along with 4 to 5 cups of water. Put on medium heat. Allow the sugar to melt and make a thick 1-strand syrup.

- Melt the pure ghee and divide it into 3 parts.

- Mix the wheat flour and water with your hand and then slowly pour it into the sugar syrup with your left hand. Keep stirring the syrup with your right hand over a medium flame.

- When the syrup and the wheat milk have mixed well together, add 1 part of the melted ghee and mix well for 5 minutes.

- Then add the second portion of the melted ghee and stir vigorously for another 5 minutes, until the mixture is thoroughly cooked and starts to thicken into a lump.

- Add the cardamom seeds, ½ teaspoon of green colour and the essence and stir for 3 minutes. Add the chopped almonds.

- Add the last portion of the ghee and stir until the halwa has become very, very thick and the ghee oozes out a little.

- Remove from the heat and place onto a greased, square aluminium tray and smoothen the surface with a greased spatula.

- Decorate with whole almonds and pistachios and allow to cool. Cut into large squares.

ZATPAT-SADO-MALIDO

(Simple Malido Cooked in a Jiffy)

200 gms. fine rava or semolina
200 gms. fine maida
500 gms. sugar
50 gms. blanched, sliced almonds
50 gms. cleaned, seedless raisins
12 egg yolks
1½ tbsps. ground cardamom and
nutmeg
1 cup milk or more as required
4 tsps. vanilla essence or pineapple
essence
Pure ghee as needed

- In a karahi, place 100 gms. of pure ghee and deep fry the sliced almonds and raisins. Set aside.

- Sieve the rava and the maida and place in a thali along with ½ cup of pure ghee and mix well. Add as much milk as is necessary to form a smooth dough. Divide the dough into 5 portions and make ¼" thick rotlis the size of a tea saucer. Pierce them with the tines of a fork.

- Put 1½ cups ghee in a karahi in which the nuts and raisins had been fried. Heat the ghee over a medium flame and fry the rotlis till red and crisp. Remove from the ghee and place in a strainer. Then break the rotlis into pieces and grind as fine as flour in a mixie.

- Place the sugar in a vessel along with 1 cup of water and allow it to melt. Heat over medium flame. Pass the sugar syrup through a muslin cloth or a fine metal sieve into an open langri or patia. Add the leftover ghee in which the rotlis had been fried to the syrup after straining it through a sieve and put the syrup to cook on medium heat until it starts to get thicker.

- Then, add the rotli which you had ground in the mixie, slowly and gradually, into the thickening syrup and stir non-stop for 10 minutes.

- Get someone to whisk the egg yolks for you as you will not be able to leave stirring the malida and whisk hard for another 10 minutes till all the yolks have been assimilated by the cooked rotli dough. Keep stirring until the ghee begins to ooze out of the malida mixture. Lower the flame and sprinkle over the cardamom-nutmeg powder. Remove from the fire and add the vanilla essence. Stir vigorously and pour the thick mixture into a fancy glass dish. Cover with the fried almond slices and raisins. If you like, you can top the malido with some coloured jujubes.

- Serve hot.

Preparation time	:	Nil
Cooking time	:	40 Mins.-1 Hr.
Serves	:	10-15

MEHSOOR PAAK

(Mysore Gram Flour Sweet)

2 cups gram flour
2 cups sugar
3¼ cup pure ghee
1½ cups water
¼ cup sliced pistachios
1 tsp. cardamom seeds

- Melt the ghee over a low fire and cool.
- Place the sugar and water in a tapeli over a medium heat and mix well till the sugar has melted. In order to remove the scum which gathers at the top, squeeze in ½ a sour lime and then strain the liquid through a muslin cloth into another large clean tapeli. Add the cardamom seeds. Place on the fire again and boil till the syrup reaches a 1-thread consistency. Remove from the fire and keep warm.
- In a clean tapeli, place the gram flour and ½ cup of melted ghee and mix well. Place on a low fire and keep stirring the flour and ghee until it becomes an ivory colour, and releases a delicious aroma.
- Replace the syrup on a medium fire and add the gram flour and mix vigorously non-stop. Wrap your right hand in a long strip of cloth and use a long handled chamach for mixing. Now comes the difficult part. Out of the 2¾ cups of melted ghee, put aside ½ a cup. You will have 2¼ cups of ghee left.
- As you mix the gram flour in the syrup, keep adding a trickle of the melted ghee from time to time. This process will take over 35 minutes or so.
- Once all the ghee is over, mix well for 3 more minutes and pour the mixture onto a greased, square, aluminium tray. Sprinkle the sliced pistachios on top.
- Boil the ½ cup of ghee which you have set aside and holding the vessel carefully, pour it carefully over the top of the Mehsoor Paak. This boiled ghee will cause holes to form in the mehsoor.
- Allow to cool. Cut neat squares whilst slightly warm because it becomes hard when cool, so cutting the pieces becomes difficult.
- Store in an airtight container. Place in the *chai-nu-loban*.

Preparation time	:	7 mins.
Cooking time	:	1 hour
Serves	:	10-12

MAAL PUWA
(Pancakes in Syrup)

This is a very popular dessert and is made in the length and breadth of India with a few minimal changes. These delicious pancakes are soaked in a syrup with rose essence. In rich households, the syrup contained saffron, which gave a golden colour and a wonderful aroma. In Parsi households, expert women would make these delicious crepe-like pancakes and place them along with the fruits and sweets for the 'afringan-farokshi' prayers or for the 'muktad' prayers. This was a rare delicacy to be had during 'muktad' days, as maal-puwas could not be made beforehand like other sweets and stored. They had to be freshly made and therefore, a nuisance during the hectic mornings, when so much effort was required by the ladies of the household to cook and present things on time. Sometimes, these pancakes were served on festival days at teatime with dollops of fresh cream obtained from the farm's buffaloes. Mostly they were topped with fried raisins and thick almond slices.

For the Syrup:

2 cups sugar
1½ cups water
1 gm. saffron or
Rose petals and ½ tsp. rose essence

For the Pancakes:

1½ cup self-raising flour
½ cup rava
1 pinch baking powder or
   soda-bi-carb
3 tbsps. sugar
1 tsp. nutmeg and cardamom
   powder
2-2½ cups milk or as necessary
2 tbsps. melted pure ghee
Ghee for frying

Preparation time	:	15 mins.
Cooking time	:	1 hour
Serves	:	10-15

- Place the sugar and water in a tapeli on medium heat. Allow to boil. Broil the saffron on an iron tava over a very low flame. Keep shifting it up and down with a piece of muslin bunched up in your right hand. You should not allow the saffron to burn. When crisp, crush it into the syrup and mix it vigorously so that the colour oozes from the saffron strands. When ready, remove from the fire and keep in a warm place.

- If the sugar is dirty, squeeze juice of half a sour lime into it. All the dirt will rise to the top. Then strain it into a clean tapeli covered by a muslin cloth.

- Take a flat – bottomed vessel. Place the rava and the self-raising flour into it. Mix in the pinch of baking powder with your fingers. Then gradually pour the milk in a trickle mixing it into the flour in circular movements with your right hand. Add the sugar and spice powder and stir until you get a smooth batter of pouring consistency. Add the melted ghee or butter, mix and keep in a warm place for at least 2 hours.

- Place a shallow frying pan on a medium flame. Place the syrup on a low flame nearby.

- Pour ghee into the frying pan until the surface is covered by at least ½" to ¾". When it becomes hot, pour in a ladleful of the batter and swirl the pan in a circular motion to get a rounded pancake, the size of a teacup saucer. With a spatula, cover the surface of the pancake with hot ghee and then turn it upside down. To be really great, maal puwa should have crisp, brown, crinkled edges and a soft, spongy centre. Do not overcook it. As soon as you feel it is done, immerse it into the hot syrup.

- Make another pancake and when it is ready, remove the first one from the syrup and serve it covered with fresh malai or rabri or fried almonds and raisins.

RABRI
(Rabdi)

One of the most wonderful ways of using up leftover milk.

2 litres of milk
1 cup sugar
¼ cup almonds, finely chopped, boiled and skinned
¼ cup pistachios, finely chopped, boiled and skinned
1 tsp. rose essence
10 pink rose petals

Preparation time	:	5 mins.
Cooking time	:	40 mins.
Serves	:	15

- Place the milk in a very large tapeli. Place it on medium heat. When the milk starts boiling, reduce the heat to low. Take a long handled chamach and stir the milk until a layer of cream is formed and push this layer on one side. Keep doing this until the milk has reduced to ½ the amount.

- Add the sugar and the finely chopped almonds and pistachios pieces and stir till an ivory colour is obtained. Remove from the fire and add the rose essence. Cool and chill.

- Serve in small individual bowls.

GOLAB-NA-GOLA
(Rosy Rounds)

450 gms. hariyali mawa
100 gms. very fine semolina or rava
300 gms. sugar
½ tsp. cardamom seeds
½ gm. saffron
Pink rose petals
Rose essence
Ghee

- Place the sugar along with 2 cups of water in a heavy bottomed pan over a medium heat. Stir and allow the mixture to boil. Make the saffron crisp on an iron tava by pushing it up and down with a tea napkin or muslin cloth in your right fist. Crumble the saffron with your fingers directly into the boiling liquid. Stir to allow the yellow colour to squeeze out of the stamens. Add the cardamom seeds. Make a one-thread syrup and remove from the fire.

- Grate the mawa and place it in a thali along with the semolina. Mash well and knead both the items into a soft, supple dough. Cover with a damp cloth and set aside for 3 to 4 hours.

- Place an iron karahi, half filled with ghee on a medium fire.

- Add 5 drops of rose essence to the kneaded mawa and knead once more for 5 minutes. The dough should be absolutely smooth.

- Make small balls out of the kneaded mawa. No cracked surfaces. The balls should be smaller than a sour lime in size.

- When the ghee heats up, lower the heat a little and put in some mawa balls and stir them gently in the ghee.

- Replace the sugar syrup on a stove on low heat.

- The balls will swell up in the ghee. Gently shift them up and down with a holed chamach till golden brown. Then lift them in the chamach, allow the extra ghee to drip in the karahi and place the balls directly into the warm syrup. Fry the balls patiently in batches. Do not try to hurry the cooking process or the rose balls will be raw inside.

- Remove the syrup from the fire and allow the balls to soak in the syrup for at least an hour.

Preparation time	:	18 mins.
Cooking time	:	45-50 mins.
Serves	:	6-9

- Serve these balls in a crystal dish. Pour some hot syrup over the balls and then sprinkle them with pink rose petals.

- These balls can be placed in the *chai-nu-loban.*

BADAM-NE-SAPARCHAN-NU-CUSTER
(Almond and Apple Custard)

1 litre full cream milk
100 gms. boiled, skinned almonds
1 large apple
½ cup cream (optional)
1 cup sugar
½ tin condensed milk
4 eggs, whisked
1 tsp. cardamom and nutmeg
    powder
1 tsp. vanilla essence

- Place the milk in a large pan or langri and bring to a boil over a medium flame. Then add the sugar and keep stirring it for 25 minutes until it becomes thick and ivory coloured. Then add the cream and the condensed milk and boil for 15 more minutes, stirring non-stop. Remove from the fire and cool.

- Take the skinned almonds and crush them in ½ cup of milk until they have been finely powdered. Add the almond milk to the sugared milk. Add the spice powder and the essence.

- Whisk the eggs well and mix into the milk.

- Cut the apple into 4 pieces. Peel and core it and cut it into thin slices.

- Pour the milk into a pyrex dish and arrange the apple slices on top of the milk. They will float on top.

- Light the oven to 350°F and bake the custard for about 45 minutes, until it becomes golden brown.

- This custard can be eaten hot or cold.

Preparation time :	35-40 mins.
Cooking time	: 45 mins.
Serves	: 8-10

FARMASOO-KHAJUR-NI-GHARI
(Date Pastry Cakes)

For the Wheat Covering:

750 gms. self-raising flour
5 tbsps. pure ghee
A pinch of salt
Rice flour
Ghee for roasting the "ghari"

For the Maan:

½ cup ghee
Rice flour, as needed

For the Date Stuffing:

400 gms. stoned, best quality, dates
75 gms. sugar or to taste
25 gms. boiled, skinned, finely
   chopped almonds
25 gms. boiled, skinned, finely
   chopped pistachios
20 gms. fried charoli
20 gms. raisins
1 tbsp. nutmeg-cardamom powder
1 tsp. rose essence

Preparation time	:	25 mins.
Cooking time	:	55 mins.
Serves	:	6

- Make the "maan" the day before you make the "gharis". Place the ghee in a large thali. Place your right hand flat on it and rotate the ghee in a circular motion. Keep on doing this until the ghee turns to cream. This may take at least 25 to 30 minutes and cannot be done in a mixie. When the ghee has become creamy and thin, add a slow trickle of rice flour and keep mixing the two in the same fashion, until you have a thick soft buttery ball of flour and ghee, which you can lift in your hand. It should be soft, not hard.

- Keep ice water in a bowl and immerse the "ball of maan" into it and refrigerate it until you use it the next day.

- The next day, place the self-raising flour, ghee and salt in a thali and rub it between your fingers for 7 minutes. Then add a trickle of water and keep kneading it to make a supple dough. Taste for salt. This covering should be slightly salty. When the dough is ready, divide it into 3 large balls.

- Take one large ball and roll it with a "velan" or rolling pin into a large rotli. Then smear the top of the whole rotli with the "maan". Sprinkle some rice flour over it and fold it into a half circle. Then smear the half with "maan" and again sprinkle some rice flour and fold it into a quarter circle. Then apply some "maan" and rice flour and fold up the quarter with your hands into a long roll. Do the same with the other 2 balls and cover them with a damp cloth and set them aside.

- I would suggest that you prepare the date filling before making the pastry, so it saves time and is cool when you handle it.

- Place the crushed, stoned dates into a thick-bottomed vessel along with the sugar and the finely chopped almonds, pistachios, charoli and raisins. Place over a low heat and gently mix the dates and sugar until the sugar has melted and the date mixture thickens. Remove from fire and allow to cool. Add the nutmeg-cardamom powder and rose essence and mix in gently.

- Cut a thick slice of dough, at least 3 inches and form into a round ball. Place it on a wooden board, sprinkled with flour. Then flatten it and roll it into a circular shape, as large as a saucer.

- Place a large tablespoon of date mixture in the center of the pastry circle and fold the dough around it to cover it completely. Press the gathered edges of the pastry circle firmly together at the top. Then, place this covered ball onto the wooden board again and flatten it from the top with the palm of your right hand, and taking the rolling pin, gently press the ball into a thick flat circle. It should not burst, so sprinkle some flour on it before rolling it gently. You should get a thick circular "ghari" at least 3" in diameter.

- Get someone to help you make the rest of the "gharis" and then place an iron tava, washed twice, on the stove on medium heat. When the tava becomes hot, wipe it with a piece of muslin soaked in a little ghee. Lower the heat and place the "ghari" in the center of the tava. Take 2 pieces of muslin in each hand and gently shift the "ghari" from side to side. You will immediately know when it is cooked from the delicious aroma which will emanate from it. With the help of a flat fish slicer, gently turn over and cook the other side. Whilst roasting it over the tava, take a teaspoon of melted ghee and pour it around the ghari, so it does not stick to the tava.

- Serve hot from the pan along with the afternoon tea. Serve the whole "ghari" to each person.

NARIEL-NA-PARIKAN
(Coconut Envelopes)

Always use best quality wheat flour when you make sweets.

For the Dough:

2 cups best quality wheat flour
1 cup maida or self-raising flour
¼ cup powdered sugar
1 tsp. cardamom-nutmeg powder
1 tbsp. curds
2 tbsps. ghee

The Coconut Filling:

1 grated coconut
1 cup sugar
Seeds of 3 cardamoms
1 tsp. vanilla essence

- Place the flour in a thali. Sprinkle the powdered sugar and spices over the flour and make a hole in the center of the heap. Place the ghee and curds in the center and gently mix into the flour. When you get a crumb-like result, pour half cup water and knead with both your hands till you get a smooth dough. Keep adding a little water at a time whilst you do your kneading. You should get a smooth, shining dough. Cover with a damp tea towel and allow to stay in a cool place for 2 hours.

- Place the coconut and sugar in a heavy-bottomed pan along with ½ cup of water. Put the vessel on a low fire and keep stirring till you get a thick syrup in which the coconut cooks till soft and done. If necessary, add more water.

- Add the cardamom seeds and cook till the coconut syrup becomes thick and sticks to the fruit. Take it off the heat.

- Add the vanilla essence and cool.

To Make the Envelopes:

- Make 4 large balls out of the dough. Roll each out into a large circle. Pat a little pure ghee on the circle and sprinkle with maida. Fold into a half moon. Apply some ghee sparingly on the flour, sprinkle with maida and fold the half moon into a quarter moon. Fold the dough into a long thick roll and place on a wooden board. Cut a slice off with a knife and roll it into a puri shape. Chop off the dough from 4 sides and make it into a square.

- Place 1 teaspoon of the sugared coconut into the center of each square. Damp the floured area around the coconut with water and carefully cover the dough with a similar sized dough square. Pat the dough down where the water had

Preparation time	:	20-25 mins.
Cooking time	:	1 hour
Serves	:	6-10

been applied, so the top cover sticks to the lower flour square.

- When all your dough or the sugared filling has been used up, place a karahi half filled with dalda or pure ghee, whichever you prefer, on the stove.

- When the ghee heats up, fry a few envelopes at a time till golden brown. Drain on kitchen paper and serve hot with tea.

MITTHA-MALAIWALA-AMLETTE
(Sweet Cream-filled Omelette)

For the Omelette:

¾ litres milk
50 gms. rava or semolina
150 gms. maida or self-raising flour
Eggs whisked
1 tsp. cardamom-nutmeg powder
1 tbsp. sugar
1 pinch salt
Pure ghee

For the Syrup:

3 cups sugar
3 cups water
1 gm. saffron

For the Topping:

400 gms. chilled, whisked malai

Preparation time	:	20 mins.
Cooking time	:	25 mins.
Serves	:	6

- Place the milk in a saucepan along with the semolina, maida, whisked eggs, spice powder, sugar, and salt. Mix well till the mixture is smooth and put in a cool place for 2 hours.

- Take a heavy bottomed large vessel and boil the sugar and water. Heat the saffron strands and crush them between your fingers in ½ cup of water.

- When the syrup comes to a boil, add the saffron liquid and simmer for 7 minutes. Remove from fire.

- Take a large iron tava and pour ghee on it. Place over a medium heat.

- Place the syrup over a very low fire.

- Pour a ladle of the omelette mixture onto the hot ghee on the tava till you get a circular omelette as large as a teacup saucer. Allow the edges to crinkle till brown and turn once. Remove after 2 minutes on a round holed chamach, and allow to soak in the warm saffron syrup for 1 minute. Do not let go the omelette from the chamach. Just carefully pull up the chamach, allow the syrup to drain off and remove onto a plate. Pour 1 tablespoon of cream over the omelette and serve hot at tea time or as an evening snack.

- If this is to be served at an important function as a dessert, sprinkle slices of almonds and pistachios over the cream.

COOVERBAI FRENCHMAN'S-DUDH-NA-PUFF
(Cooverbai Frenchman's Milk Puffs)

This can only be made in the cool months.

One of the best liquid sweets that the Parsis made was the dudh-na-puff. It consisted of a tall glass of lacy milk, sweet and chilled. You had to eat the lacy cream the glass contained with a spoon. During the day, the milk – thick and creamy – was cooked with sugar and then cooled. At night, the vessel in which it was made was covered tightly with fine muslin and kept on the terrace to chill. Maybe the cold dew had something to do with making the puffs taste great. But, by 5.30 to 6 a.m., the vessel was brought into the house. My mother was set to churn the milk with an egg beater by my grandmother. The froth which arose from the churning, was then removed, spoon by spoon, into tall glasses. To eat them was a delight. I am giving this simple recipe below.

2 litres full cream milk
1¾ cups of sugar
1 tsp. nutmeg-cardamom powder
1 tsp. vanilla essence

- Boil the milk in a large langri over a low fire. Bring it to a boil, stirring all the time. Do so 4 times. Cool. Add the nutmeg-cardamom powder and the vanilla essence. Stir.

- In the night, cover the mouth of the vessel tightly with a large piece of mulmul. Then, put the vessel on your terrace or verandah the whole night through.

- By 6 a.m., take the vessel into the house. Place it on a table in your kitchen. Then take an egg beater and whisk it briskly. Froth will form on top of the milk. With a spoon, collect it and fill 6 to 8 tall glasses.

- Chill the glasses in your refrigerator and serve at breakfast time.

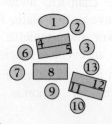

Tea Tray   (1)
Egg and Saffron Ravo   (2)
Homai Nalladaru's
Mawa Coconut Barfi   (3)
Mawa Samosas   (4)
Coconut Chaptis   (5)
Red Chikkat Halwa   (6)
Mehsoor Pak   (7)

Chapat or Pancakes   (8)
Half Moon Crescents
Stuffed with Coconut   (9)
Bhakhras   (10)
Date Ghari   (11)
Dal Poli   (12)
Mango – Saffron Murambo
(Marmalade)   (13)

GULAB-NI-CHINA-GHAS-NI-JELLY
(Rose China Grass Jelly)

150 gms. china grass, cut into
    small pieces
1 litre creamy milk
6 tbsps. rose syrup
¾ cup sugar
Pink rose petals

Preparation time	:	12 mins.
Cooking time	:	30 mins.
Serves	:	6

- Place the china grass pieces in 1 cup of water in a saucepan over a slow heat and allow to simmer until they are totally dissolved in the water.

- Heat the milk and sugar and pour in the dissolved china grass and allow to simmer for 10 minutes. Strain the milk into a clean vessel and add the rose syrup and mix vigorously till you get a pale pink colour and an essence of roses from the milk.

- Pour into a clear glass bowl, cover with foil and chill overnight. The next day, decorate with pale pink rose petals before serving it.

GOSASP MEHTA-NU-CONDENSED-DUDH-NU-DAHI
(Gosasp Mehta's Yogurt made with Condensed Milk)

1½ litres full cream milk
1 whole tin condensed milk
100 gms. yogurt for starters

Preparation time	:	5 mins.
Cooking time	:	15 mins.
Serves	:	4-8

- Heat the milk and bring it to a boil. Remove from the fire and add the tin of condensed milk and mix well.

- Heat the milk for 2 to 3 minutes and cool.

- Tie the yogurt starter in a piece of mulmul and allow any water in it to seep out.

- Apply the yogurt to the inner side of the dish or bowl you will be using to make the yogurt. If any remains, mix it into the milk.

- Then heat your oven at 350°F for 5 minutes. Shut it off.

- Pour the milk into the dish or bowl and put it into the oven. Leave it till it sets. Allow to chill in the refrigerator overnight.

- Decorate the top with sliced pistachios, almonds and crisp stamens of saffron.

Katy Dalal's Vegetable
Khichri (1)
Bharuchi Lobster Patia (2)

BADAM-NA-MAKROOM
(Almond Macaroons)

Make these by using up the egg whites left over from the Eda Paak. Keep the egg whites of 8 eggs separate from the beginning.

1 kg. almonds
1 kg. sugar
8 tbsps. powdered sugar
8 egg whites
2 tsps. vanilla or almond essence

- Boil and skin the almonds and allow them to dry.

- Grind them fine in your mixer.

- Mix the powdered sugar and the ground almonds and the essence. Then add the 8 egg whites, heavily whisked. Mix until the almonds and egg whites are light and well mixed.

- Put the oven at 150°F to 170°F.

- Place butter paper on a tray and grease it. Then put tiny dollops of the mixture in neat lines, 2" away from each other, and bake in the oven till firm.

Preparation time	:	20 mins.
Cooking time	:	25-30 mins.
Serves	:	8-10

KERA-NE-KISMIS-NA-KARKARIA
(Banana And Raisin Fritters)

4 ripe bananas
1½ cups sugar
1½ cups wheat flour
½ cup rava or semolina
3 eggs
1½ tsps. cardamom and nutmeg
   powder
1½ tsps. vanilla essence
1 tbsp. raisins
1 tbsp. charoli
Ghee

- Place the sugar and 1 tablespoon ghee in a deep vessel or large round bowl.

- Add 3 whisked eggs to the sugar and cream it with a spoon until the sugar melts.

- Gradually add the flour and rava and mix well. Then add the bananas well mashed, the spice powder and vanilla essence and mix well. Add raisins and charoli. Set in a warm place for 2 hours.

- Place a karahi half filled with ghee on a medium flame. When hot, put in a few tablespoons of the mixture. The fritters will swell in the hot ghee. Allow them to become golden brown on both sides. Remove on paper napkins.

- Serve hot at tea time.

Preparation time	:	35-40 mins.
Cooking time	:	25 mins.
Serves	:	4-6

SANTRA-JELLY-THI-BHARELA

(Oranges Stuffed with Jelly)

A huge favourite with Bombay Parsis, 50 years ago.

12 very large ripe oranges
2 tbsps. gelatine
½ litre milk
½ cup sugar
25 gms. China grass
1 tsp. vanilla essence
12 cherries, canned

- Take the oranges and with a very sharp knife, slice the tops. Remove the pulp with a very sharp, thin knife, taking care not to cut the skin. Make juice from the pulp and sieve the juice through a piece of muslin.

- Place the gelatine in ½ cup of water and melt it over a low flame. When thoroughly melted, mix it into the orange juice and pour into a flat square tray. Chill overnight. Cover with foil.

- Keep the empty orange shells in the refrigerator to use them the next day.

- Melt the China grass in ½ cup of water over a low fire.

- Place the milk and sugar in a tapeli over a medium fire. Keep stirring the mixture until it reduces a little in quantity. Then add the melted China grass and cook the milk for 5 minutes more. Remove from the fire, add the vanilla essence and cool. Pour into a square tray and chill overnight in the refrigerator. Cover with foil.

- The next day, prepare 10 quarter plates with 10 teaspoons. Place the empty orange shells, one in each plate.

- As soon as lunch is over, take a helper with yourself into the kitchen.

- Cut both the jellies into small ¾" squares. Fill each orange half with orange jelly and half with white China grass jelly squares. Top each orange dessert with a cherry. Serve immediately.

- This is a cool and delicious dessert.

Preparation time	:	25 mins.
Cooking time	:	40 mins.
Serves	:	10

SAKARKAND-NI-ROTLI
(Sweet Potato Stuffed Rotlis)

1 cup best quality wheat flour
½ cup self-raising flour
5 big fat sweet potatoes
1 cup sugar
1 tsp. vanilla essence
1 tsp. nutmeg-cardamom powder
1 pinch of salt
Pure ghee

- Place the 2 flours and salt in a thali. Add ½ cup of ghee and mix well. Then slowly add a little water at a time till you have a soft, supple and smooth dough. Cover with a damp cloth whilst you cook the sweet potato stuffing.

- Boil or steam the sweet potatoes in a pressure cooker. Cool them, skin them and mash them.

- Place 2 tablespoons of pure ghee in a langri over a medium flame. When it becomes hot, add the sweet potatoes and the sugar. Lower the flame and mix non-stop till the sugar has melted and you have a soft sweet potato dough. Remove from the fire and cool. Add the vanilla essence and the nutmeg-cardamom powder and knead the sweet potato well.

- Take a large round of wheat dough. Make a thick puri and stuff it with the sweet potato and cover the mixture well like a pattice. Then sprinkle some ata or dry flour on a wooden board and cover the pattice on both sides lightly with the flour, and then take a velan or rolling pin and very gently roll it out the size of a saucer.

- You should get at least 6 to 10 large rounds of dough.

- Place an iron tava on the fire at medium heat. Wipe it with a damp cloth and place one stuffed rotli upon it. Move it from side to side and flip it over and do the same again. Now flip it over the second time and trickle a little melted ghee around its circumference and shake it from side to side. Cook the other side in the same manner till golden red. Remove from the fire.

- Serve hot at breakfast or tea time.

Preparation time	:	12 mins.
Cooking time	:	35-45 mins.
Serves	:	6

fish

TARELA-SOOKKA-BOOMLA

(Dried Fried Bombay Ducks)

16 large dried Bombay Ducks
A pinch of salt

- Clean the Bombay Ducks by cutting off their heads, fins and tails. Take a very sharp knife and cut the stomach portion and clean it well. Soak in luke warm water for 20 minutes. After the time is up, pluck the flesh with your fingers in fine shreds. Throw away the central bone. Lightly wipe the soaked flesh with a piece of soft muslin and dry well. If liked you can place the shreds at a low temperature in the oven to dry up for a few minutes.

- Heat a karahi with sesame oil. Do not use too much oil as it will be wasted ultimately. Place it on a medium flame. When it gets hot, sprinkle the shredded Bombay Ducks with very little fine salt and place it in the hot oil in small batches, so the pieces have enough place to float around in the hot oil and separate easily and become crisp. The oil should not get black because of too much heat. Lower the flame a little and control the heat.

- My family likes this method of dried, fried Bombay Ducks the best.

Preparation time	:	30 mins.
Cooking time	:	15 mins.
Serves	:	4-6

BHUNJELA SOOKKA BOOMLA
(Dry Roasted Dried Bombay Ducks)

18 large dried Bombay Ducks

- The best method of cooking dried Bombay Ducks was to clean them by cutting off heads, fins and tails and cutting and cleaning the stomach portions.

- My great grandmother Soonamai would place the dried ducks under white hot embers of the wooden fire on which she cooked. She would turn them once or twice, test them for crispness by banking them against a wooden board and serve them whole with toddy, hot drinks or food. If there was no time to make a meal because of various problems, she would serve these Bombay Ducks with yellow dal, white rice and pickles or serve them with a vegetable khichdi and pickles.

- When I joined the Ripon Club as its caterer in 1982 or 1983, I am not sure which year, the then Secretary, the late Mr. Pochkhanawalla, taught me how to get almost the same results, by baking them in an electric oven.

- Do try your hand at placing them on a tray and baking at 300° F till they are crisp. Turn them up and down twice.

Preparation time	:	7 mins.
Cooking time	:	App. 10 mins.
Serves	:	4-6

DRIED BOMBAY DUCK PATIA WITH
RED PUMPKIN AND BANANAS

30 large dried Bombay Ducks,
   cleaned and
   cut into 4 pieces each
150 gms. red pumpkin, skinned and
   chopped
3 large green bananas, skinned and
   sliced
2 large whole garlic pods ⎤
2 tbsps. cumin seeds   ⎥
12-15 large kashmiri   ⎬ Grind
   chillies, deseeded   finely
1 tsp. mustard seeds   ⎥
1 tbsp. turmeric powder ⎦
1½ cups sugarcane vinegar
1 cup crushed jaggery
Coarse salt
Sesame seed oil

Preparation time	:	25 mins.
Cooking time	:	35-45 mins.
Serves	:	6-8

- After you have removed the mouth, fins and tail of the dried Bombay Ducks, scrape the skin lightly to remove the scales. Cut each into 4 pieces and soak them for an hour. Then wash them and remove the bones.

- Grind the masala till soft with the help of the vinegar.

- Pour ½ cup of oil into a kalai patia or any other heavy based vessel. Place over medium heat. When hot, add the masala and fry for 3 to 5 minutes till red hot and then add the deboned, washed, Bombay Ducks. Lower the flame, stir gently and cook over a low fire for 10 minutes. Add the vinegar and Jaggery. Do not add salt unless you have tasted the fish as it has been soaked in salt and then dried.

- Cook the red pumpkin with a little salt and pinch of turmeric in 1 cup water till soft. Add it to the fish along with the sliced bananas and cook till the gravy has dried.

- Serve with rice rotlis or khichdi.

JABARJAST-THALI-CHHAMNO-KOLMI-BHARELO
(Large Thali Pomfret stuffed with Prawns)

1 very large thali pomfret
1½ tbsp. black pepper
1½ tbsp. turmeric powder
2 tbsp. chilli powder

Prawn Stuffing:

150 gms. shelled, deveined, washed
    prawns
½ tsp. turmeric
4 kashmiri chillies,
    deseeded
5 black peppercorns
1 tsp. poppy seeds
1 tsp. sesame seeds
2 tsps. sugar
Salt to taste
Sesame oil

} Grind to a paste in sugarcane vinegar

* Clean the huge pomfret carefully. It will be greasy. Place on a newspaper on the cutting board. Leave the whole fish intact. Do not remove the fins or tail, but clean them with the edge of a knife. Remove both the gills carefully and then cut across the side of the stomach where the arrows are and remove the intestines, liver and any fish eggs there may be. Wash thoroughly, twice with wheat flour, and the third time with clear water. Squeeze juice from 3 large sour limes. First apply salt and black pepper powder all over the fish and into the stomach cavity and then cover it with the lime juice. Put some juice inside the stomach cavity also. Place the pomfret onto a large thali and allow to marinade for 2 hours. Turn it over every half an hour so that it saturates well in the lime juice. Apply chilli powder and turmeric powder lavishly on both sides.

* You may then stuff it with the prawns. These prawns should be cooked dry. (See last para of recipe). Gravy will make it difficult to stuff the pomfret. After you have stuffed it, pack it up by tying it with a thin, white string.

* Take a huge, iron tava and put it on the fire. Pour sesame oil generously on the tava and allow to heat well. Place both the tavathas or long-handled slicers in the hot oil so that they do not stick to the pomfret skin if cold.

* Keep a silver salver ready. Decorate its edges with pineapple slices on top of lettuce (endive) leaves. Cut flowers out of papayas and sweet limes. If you can make a basket out of a watermelon, serrate the edges, and fill the watermelon with sweets and chocolates. Place finely cut green cabbage washed in water in the centre.

Preparation time	:	20-25 mins.
Cooking time	:	40-50 mins.
Serves	:	4-6

- Fry the pomfret carefully. Lower the flame and allow it to cook fully for 12 to 15 minutes on each side. First, cook one side and then the other. Finally, lower it carefully onto the centre of the salver. Accompany it with mango pickle, ghee rice and toovar dal with a vaghar of fried onions, fried finely sliced garlic, raw green chillies, deseeded and cut in thin slices, and freshly chopped coriander. Serve any extra leftover prawns also.

- Place the prawns, ground paste and 2 table-spoons of oil in a saucepan and cover over a low heat, stirring the prawns from side to side. Sprinkle a little water now and then, so the prawns become tender. Dry up the masala. Leave no gravy.

TATRELI KOLMI
(Sautéed Prawns)

30 large tiger prawns, deveined
4 green chillies, deseeded
8 Kashmiri chillies,
   deseeded
20 cashew nuts   Grind fine in lime juice
9 large cloves garlic
1 tbsp. cumin
1 tsp. aniseeds
½ cup coriander leaves
1" piece turmeric
2 onions, cut into halves
   and thinly sliced
1 tbsp. grated ginger
½ tsp. mustard seeds
1 green mango, skinned
   and cut julienne (if in season)
Salt, Sesame oil

- Wash the prawns twice, put salt and coat with the ground masala and keep aside for 2 hours.

- Take a flat bottomed vessel. Pour in half a cup of oil and place on medium heat. Crush the sliced onions and add it to the oil along with the mustard seeds and curry leaves.

- Stir and half cook the onions and then add the prawns. Mix well, cover the prawns and cook over a low fire. When three-quarters cooked, add the mango strips if using them. Cook till tender. Taste for salt.

- Serve with hot drinks or as a starter.

Preparation time	:	15 mins.
Cooking time	:	22 mins.
Serves	:	6

TAJA-RANDHELA-CHHAMNA

(Fresh Pomfrets cooked in Gravy)

2 Pomfrets, each cut into 4 slices
   and washed twice
250 gms. finely chopped onions
½ cup tamarind pulp
½ cup jaggery, crushed
1 pod garlic, medium sized,
   skinned and finely chopped
1 bunch fresh coriander ⎤ Finely
3 green chillies, deseeded ⎦ chopped
1 bunch fresh coriander ⎤ Finely
3 green chillies deseeded ⎦ ground
1 tsp. turmeric powder
1 tsp. black pepper powder
1½ tsp. Parsi dhansakh masala
Salt, Sesame oil

Preparation time	:	7-10 mins.
Cooking time	:	20-25 mins.
Serves	:	4-6

- Place the chopped onions in a patia along with half a cup of oil and cook till soft and pink over a low fire, along with the garlic.

- Meanwhile, salt the fish. Then apply the ground coriander and chillies to the slices. After this, add the chopped chillies and coriander and the turmeric, black pepper and dhansakh powders. Mix into the fish by hand.

- Add water, about 2 cups, and allow the fish to come to a boil.

- Melt the jaggery in the tamarind pulp and add to the fish gravy. Shake the pan from side to side. Remove from the fire once the fish is cooked.

- Serve with white rice, papads and sweet carrot pickle.

SARKA-MA-TAJI-MACCHI-NO-PATIO

450 gms. shelled, deveined washed
   prawns or any other fresh fish

2 garlic pods, whole,
   skinned

2 large onions, skinned

1" piece fresh turmeric   Grind

8-10 kashmiri chillies,   in a
   deseeded   little

½ teacup fresh coriander,   water
   chopped

5 black peppercorns

1 tbsp. cumin seeds

2 slit green chillies, deseeded

2 sprigs curry leaves

1¼ cup sugarcane vinegar

Coarse salt, Peanut oil

Preparation time	:	15 mins.
Cooking time	:	20 mins.
Serves	:	4-6

- Add coarse salt to the washed prawns or fish. Allow to marinade for ½ hour.

- Grind all the masala until fine and place it in a heavy bottomed patia which has good kalai on it. Or use a heavy stainless steel vessel with a copper bottom or a non-stick karahi.

- Add the vinegar and ½ cup of oil to the pan with the masala and mix well.

- Mix the salted prawns or fish into the masala and coat the fish well with it. Place the vessel on a medium flame and allow it to boil. Hold the vessel with pot holders in both your hands and shake well. Lower the flame and allow to simmer for 5 minutes.

- Serve hot with rotlis or khichdi.

BHILAVA KASHMIRI
MARCHA-NA-MASALA-MA-TATRELA
(Baby Pomfrets fried in Kashmiri Chilli Masala)

8-10 baby pomfrets
1 tbsp. turmeric
8-10 Kashmiri chillies,
   deseeded ⎤
16 large cloves garlic
1 tbsp. broiled coriander
   seeds
1 tbsp. broiled cumin seeds ⎬ Grind with vinegar
2 tbsps. sesame seeds
10 black peppercorns
1 cup chopped coriander
   leaves ⎦
Salt
Sesame oil

- Clean the baby pomfrets, remove the gills, wash twice and keep whole. Make 2 cuts on the body and do not cut off the tail. Salt them, apply turmeric and set aside.

- Grind the masala very fine and apply it to the pomfrets and marinade them for 30 minutes.

- Heat a large iron tava with sesame oil and when the oil is smoking hot, reduce the heat and fry the pomfrets in small batches till golden red and done.

- Serve directly from pan to table along with black masoor, chana dar, val dar or mung dar and rotlis.

Preparation time	:	10 mins.
Cooking time	:	20 mins.
Serves	:	6

BHILAVA-NO-RAS

8 Bhilavas or Baby pomfrets whole
8-10 green chillies, deseeded ⎤
12 large cloves garlic
1½ tbsps. cumin seeds
1 tsp. mustard seeds ⎬ Grind fine
5 black peppercorns
4 tbsps. grated coconut
2 large onions, chopped ⎦
¼ cup tamarind pulp ⎤ Mix
¼ cup crushed jaggery ⎦ (Optional)
2 sprigs curry leaves
Salt
Sesame oil

- Clean and wash the baby pomfrets inside out twice. Salt them and set aside.

- Grind the masala along with the onions.

- Take a large, open mouthed vessel and place on a medium heat. Add the curry leaves and the masala and lower the heat and cook for 5 minutes. Add 2 litres of water and salt and allow to come to a boil on high heat. Add the baby pomfrets and cook on high for 6 minutes and then add the mixed tamarind and jaggery. Lower the flame and simmer for 5 minutes more. Taste for salt.

- Serve with white rice, papads and mango pickle in oil.

Preparation time	:	10 mins.
Cooking time	:	20 mins.
Serves	:	6

GOR-AMLI-NA-RAS-MA-PATRA-NI-MACCHI

(Patra Fish cooked in a Tamarind-Jaggery Sauce)

12 pieces or fillets of pomfret,
   surmai, ravas
   or ghol fish
12 banana leaves, washed and dried
Juice of 3 sour limes
1½ tsps. black pepper powder
1 tsp. turmeric powder
1 coconut, freshly grated
1 large bunch coriander
   leaves only
8 green chillies, deseeded
12 large garlic cloves
1 tbsp. cumin seeds
15 black peppercorns
Salt

} Grind fine with a little water

1 cup tamarind pulp
1 cup smashed jaggery
½ tsp. turmeric powder
½ tsp. chilli powder
½ cup finely chopped fresh
   coriander leaves
1 tsp. freshly grated ginger
2 sprigs curry leaves
Salt
Peanut oil

Preparation time	: 25 mins.
Cooking time	: 35 mins.
Serves	: 6-8

- Grind the green chutney very fine and reserve any water from the mixie or stone quern.

- Wash the fish twice and marinade in salt, black pepper powder and turmeric powder for 2 hours.

- Take a deep broad vessel. Put in 1 tablespoon of oil and place on medium heat. Add the grated ginger and curry leaves, stir for a minute and add the turmeric and chilli powders and 1 cup of water. When the mixture comes to a boil, add the tamarind pulp, jaggery and salt and allow to simmer for 10 minutes. Remove from the fire.

- Cut the banana leaf according to your requirements. Normally 2 to 4 pieces of fish are bundled from 1 large leaf. Place the leaf on a wooden board. Cover the fish with the hot green chutney and wrap it up carefully into a neat parcel. No fish or chutney should be seen. Then tie the package with a thin white string.

- When all the fish packages are ready, take a large thali or kathrot. Apply a thin film of oil on its bottom and arrange the pieces in it. Place on a medium heat and pour the hot tamarind-jaggery gravy over the pieces. Cover tightly with a well fitting lid or foil and allow to simmer for 12 to 15 minutes, turning the fish over once.

- Serve with dhan-dal or plain white rice or khichdi. Use the gravy as patia.

LARGE FRIED SURMAI SLICES

6 large slices, surmai fish
8-10 red Kashmiri chillies ⎤
10 large cloves garlic ⎥ Grind
1 tbsp. cumin seeds ⎥ in a
6 black pepper corns ⎥ little
1½ tbsp. sesame seeds ⎥ vinegar
1½ tbsp. turmeric powder ⎦
Salt
Til oil

Preparation time	:	10 mins.
Cooking time	:	20 mins.
Serves	:	6

- Wash the fish slices and marinade them in salt and the turmeric powder.

- Grind the masala fine and then apply it to the slices. Keep for 2 hours.

- Heat oil in a black iron tava or large skillet. When hot, fry the slices 3 or 4 at a time, till well done.

- Serve with lime wedges along with any thick dal and rotlis.

BANGRA-NI-KARI

(Mackerel Curry)

10 fresh large bangras
Milk of 1 whole coconut ⎤
2 tbsps. broiled coriander ⎥
   seeds ⎥ Grind
1 tbsp. broiled cumin seeds ⎥ fine
12 Kashmiri or Goa chillies ⎬ with
Tamarind, the size of ⎥ water
   2 sour limes ⎥
1 grated large onion ⎦
4 kokum fruits
3 green chillies, slit
Salt

Preparation time	:	18 mins.
Cooking time	:	30-35 mins.
Serves	:	6

- Cut the bangras in half – fry the upper half as you wish. Wash the lower halves well and salt them and set aside. If you like, use the whole bangra.

- Prepare the masala very fine and place in a large patia. Add 1 cup of water and mix well with the masala and bring to a boil. Add a little salt and the coconut milk (at least 3 cups) and slit green chillies. When the curry begins to boil, add the washed kokum fruit and the bangras. Allow to boil well for 5 minutes. Remove from fire.

- Serve with boiled white rice and papads.

BHARUCHI-SONDH (LOBSTER)-NO-PATIO

1 kg. lobster tails, deveined
3 large onions, chopped fine
2 bunches spring onions, chopped fine till 6 inches above the roots
2 bunches fresh garlic ⎫
1 large garlic pod ⎪ Grind
12 green chillies, deseeded ⎬ fine
2" fresh green turmeric ⎪ with a little
15 black peppercorns ⎪ water
2 tbsps. cumin seeds ⎭
1 bunch fresh coriander
30 green pickled peppercorns
Salt
Pure ghee

- Wash the lobster tails 3 times. Check that the veins have been properly removed. Salt and allow to marinade in a cool place for at least 1 hour.

- Chop the coriander leaves after washing them. Use the tender stem.

- Chop the spring onions into fine rings and cut the dried onions fine. Chop the green garlic after removing the long roots and washing the slender green shoots.

- Grind the masala till soft on a stone queen. Retain the masala water.

- Apply all the ground masala to the lobsters and keep aside for 30 minutes.

- Place 4 tablespoons pure ghee in a large langri and place on a medium fire. Fry the onions till soft and pink. Add the spring onions and freshly chopped green garlic and cook over a low heat.

- Add the lobsters along with the masala it was marinaded in and fry and turn gently several times in the langri. After 5 minutes, add a cup of hot water and the pickled green peppercorns and cook gently till soft. If necessary, add some more hot water. Taste for salt.

- You can serve this dish with rotlis, parathas, white ghee rice or a vegetable pulao with tomato chutney on the side.

Preparation time	:	35-40 mins.
Cooking time	:	45-55 mins.
Serves	:	8

Thali Pomfert Stuffed with Prawns

KOLMI, SEKTA-NI-SING, NE-KACHHI-KERI-NE-KOHRA-NU-DOHRU

(Prawn, Drumstick, Raw Mango and Pumpkin Gravy)

400 gms. boiled pumpkin, crushed
300 gms. shelled, deveined, washed
   prawns
6 drumsticks, skinned and cut into
   3" pieces and tied into bundles
4 tender mangoes, skinned and cut
   into 4 pieces each
100 gms. freshly grated
   coconut ⎤
8 Kashmiri chillies, deseeded ⎟ Grind
10 large cloves ⎟ in a
1½" piece of fresh turmeric ⎬ little
1" piece ginger ⎟ water
½ cup finely chopped
   coriander ⎦
½ cup crushed jaggery
2 sprigs curry leaves
Salt
Sesame (Til) oil

Preparation time	:	18 mins.
Cooking time	:	35 mins.
Serves	:	6

- Wash the prawns and marinade them in salt and set aside.

- Boil the mangoes and the jaggery in 1 cup of water and set aside.

- Boil the drumstick bundles in turmeric and salt water.

- Put the onions along with 3 tablespoons of sesame oil and the curry leaves into a patia. Place the vessel over a medium flame and cook the onions till they are soft.

- Add the ground masala and cook till a good aroma arises from the pan. Then add the prawns. Lower the flame and allow them to simmer in the masala for 5 minutes, after which add the crushed pumpkin. Allow to simmer for 10 minutes over a very low flame. When the prawns are tender, add the boiled mangoes along with the water, the crushed jaggery and the drumstick bundles. Stir and taste for salt.

- Serve with khichdi and papads.

Baby Pomfrets in Gravy (1)
Masala Chops (2)
Prawns Cooked in
Butter with Tomatoes (3)

MOTTI-KOLMI-PAKELI-KERI-SATHE

(Tiger Prawns Cooked In Ripe Mangoes)

10 large tiger prawns
4 Alphonso mangoes
8 baby onions and 4 small onions,
   sliced
1½" piece ginger
4 green chillies, slit into 4,
   deseeded with stem
¼ tsp. sesame seeds
¼ tsp. mustard seeds
½ tsp. coriander seeds
½ tsp. turmeric powder
1 tsp. Kairi sambhar masala
1 tsp. East Indian Bottle masala
Juice of 2 sour limes
1 large tomato, skinned and
   chopped
3 stems curry leaves
Coarse salt
Sesame seed oil

- Cut the tiger prawns just above the eyes and leave the rest of the shell on. Remove the shell on its back and de-vein. Wash gently twice, so that the shell remains intact and does not fall off.

- Marinade the prawns in coarse salt, the lime juice and turmeric powder for 2 hours.

- Skin the baby onions and cut the onions into thin slices. Separate the rings.

- Take a large langri or any other flat-bottomed vessel or a large karahi in which the 10 tiger prawns will fit in comfortably.

- Pour in ½ cup of sesame oil and place on medium heat.

- When the oil becomes hot, lower the heat a little and put in the coriander seeds, mustard seeds and the curry leaves and allow them to crackle and splutter.

- Add the sliced onions and stir for 2 minutes. Then add the prawns and lay them comfortably on the cooking onions. Stir gently, up and down, and then sprinkle over the Kairi sambhar and the East India Bottle masalas.

- Add the split green chillies and tomatoes. Lower the heat to very low and cover and allow the prawns to cook in their own juice.

- Skin the ripe mangoes. Cut each cheek into 4 pieces. You will get 32 pieces in all. Sprinkle a little fine salt on them and add them to the cooking prawns. Stir gently. Do not bruise the pieces. Cover and allow to simmer with the prawns for 10 minutes.

- Remove from the fire and serve immediately with a vegetable khichdi or paratha.

- These prawns would be an excellent accompaniment to vegetables or dars.

Preparation time	:	15-18 mins.
Cooking time	:	30-35 mins.
Serves	:	4-6

SOOKI-MASALA-NI-KOLMI

(Dry Cooked Masala Prawns)

500 gms. large prawns, keep intact, from behind the eyes and shell the back and devein it, wash twice

¼ grated coconut
10 Kashmiri chillies, deseeded
10 large cloves garlic
1 tbsp. garam masala
2 tbsps. broken cashew nuts
1 tbsp. broiled dhania
1 large fine cut onion
} Grind in a little vinegar

1 cup dahi, whisked
½ tsp. mustard seeds
2 sprigs curry leaves
Salt, Sesame oil

Preparation time	:	20 mins.
Cooking time	:	30-35 mins.
Serves	:	4-6

- Mix the prawns into the masala and whisked curds and keep for 2 hours.

- Place a langri on a medium flame with 3 table-spoons of oil. When it heats up, add the mustard seeds and curry leaves. When they crackle, add the masala prawns and lower the flame and cook the prawns in their own juice. Cover and allow to simmer till soft. If necessary, add 2 tablespoons of water at a time till prawns are soft.

- Serve with rice rotlis.

KOLMI-NE-LILA LASAN-NU-CHOBUTT

(Prawn and Fresh Garlic Mixture)

400 gms. shelled, deveined prawns
3 bunches of green garlic
6 large onions, cut into half, sliced and deep fried
12 black pepper corns
1 tbsp. jeera
1 tsp. turmeric powder
1 tsp. red chilli powder
6 green chillies, deseeded
} Grind in a little water

Salt
Ghee

Preparation time	:	5 mins.
Cooking time	:	35 mins.
Serves	:	4-6

- Wash the prawns, marinade them in salt and set aside.

- Clean the tiny white hairlike grass at the end of the garlic. Wash and chop finely and set aside.

- Place ½ cup of ghee in a vessel and when hot, fry the ground masala in it for a few minutes. Add the prawns and cover and allow to cook over a low heat. When the prawns have softened, add the chopped green garlic and stir the prawns up and down till the garlic has softened. Then finely fold in the fried onions. Stir gently, simmer for 5 minutes and serve with hot rotlis.

- Sprinkle a little water, if necessary.

KHORSHED BANOO PATEL NI
SANDOVELI KOLMI PAPETA-KANDA SATHE

(Khorshed Banoo Patel's Marinaded Prawns with Potatoes and Onions)

500 gms. deveined prawns,
   washed twice
3 large onions, chopped fine
2 medium potatoes,
   chopped into ½" cubes
1 tbsp. ground ginger-garlic
2 tsps. turmeric powder
1 tbsp. red chilli powder
2 tsps. cumin seeds
Salt
Sesame oil

Preparation time	:	25 mins.
Cooking time	:	20-25 mins.
Serves	:	4-8

- Place the prawns, onions and potato pieces and salt in a vessel. Mix in the ginger-garlic paste and the turmeric and chilli powders. Crush the whole lot with your right hand and allow to keep in a cool place for 2 hours.

- Place ¾ cup oil in a patia. Allow to heat over a medium flame. Crush the cumin seeds between the palms of your hands and add them to the hot oil.

- Stir the cumin for 1 minute and add the marinaded prawns, onions and potatoes to the oil and mix briskly for 5 minutes. Then lower the flame and cover and cook till prawns and potatoes are tender. Add water only if necessary.

- Serve with rotlis or khichri.

KHORSHED BANOO PATEL NI MASALA-NI-KOLMI

(Khorshed Banoo Patel's Masala Prawns)

1 kg. deveined prawns, washed
   twice
1 tbsp. turmeric powder
6 split green chillies, deseeded
100 gms. jaggery
Sugarcane vinegar
50 gms. Kashmiri chillies,
   deseeded   ⎤
300 gms. large cloves garlic ⎬ Grind in vinegar
70 gms. cumin seeds |
1 tbsp. black mustard seeds ⎦
3 sprigs curry leaves
Salt, Sesame oil

Preparation time	:	20 mins.
Cooking time	:	35 mins.
Serves	:	6-8

- Add salt and turmeric powder to the prawns and set aside in a cool place.

- Place ½ cup of oil in a large patia over a medium heat. Add the curry leaves and when they start crackling, put in the ground masala and the green split chillies and mix well. Cook over a low flame for 5 minutes. Add the prawns and allow them to cook in their own juice for 7 minutes. Then add 2 cups of vinegar and cook till tender.

- Pound the jaggery and sprinkle over the prawns when they have become soft and mix well. Allow the gravy in the prawns to dry up before removing the prawns from the fire.

- Serve with a dal or vegetables with hot rotlis.

MAKHAN-MA-RANDHELI-KOLMI-NE-TAMBOTU

(Prawns cooked in Butter with Tomatoes)

300 gms. prawns, shelled, deveined
  and washed
2 large onions, finely chopped
6 red tomatoes, skinned
2 green chillies, deseeded
¼ coconut, grated   ⎤ Grind
1 tbsp. poppy seeds   ⎟ fine in
6 Kashmiri chillies, deseeded   ⎬ a little
1" piece fresh turmeric   ⎟ water
2 tsps. sugar   ⎦
Salt
2 tbsps. white butter, unsalted
1 tbsp. Peanut oil

Preparation time	:	15 mins.
Cooking time	:	35-40 mins.
Serves	:	4-6

• Heat the oil in a vessel over a very low heat. Add the butter and the onions and cook over low heat. Cover so that the onions cook quickly in their own steam.

• Salt the washed prawns and set aside.

• When the onions are soft and pink, add the ground masala and fry for 5 minutes. Then add the salted prawns. Stir for 5 minutes.

• Cut each skinned tomato into 6 pieces and add to the prawns and cover and keep over low heat till the prawns are cooked. Add water to the lid and when necessary, add it to the pan so that the prawns soften and get cooked faster. Sprinkle over the green chillies and the sugar, mix well, and serve hot with wheat flour rotlis.

MAKHAN-LILA MARCHAN-NE-RAI-MA-KOLMI

(Prawns cooked in Butter, Green Chillies and Mustard Seeds)

28 very large prawns, deveined
  and washed
6 green chillies, split and deseeded
Juice of 3 sour limes
1 tsp. mustard seeds
1 tsp. broiled coriander seeds
Coarse salt
Butter
Oil

Preparation time	:	20 mins.
Cooking time	:	25 mins.
Serves	:	4

• Wash the prawns twice and marinade in the lime juice and salt for 2 hours.

• Gently heat 1¼ cup butter and ¼ cup oil in a large vessel. When it heats up, add the mustard seeds, allow to crackle, lower heat and add the green split chillies and the broiled coriander seeds. Mix for one minute and add the prawns reserving the lime juice.

• Stir the prawns up and down and allow to cook in their own juice. When they show signs of the juice drying up, and the prawns are still not tender, add half a cup of water and the leftover lime juice. Cover and cook till tender.

• Arrange in a flat dish and decorate with iceberg lettuce, red radishes and lemon wedges.

TOORIYA-MA-TIKKHI-KOLMI

(Hot Ridge Gourd with Prawns)

700 gms. skinned ridge gourd
   cut into fine thin pieces
350 gms. prawns, skinned and
   deveined and washed
2 large onions, finely chopped
2 large tomatoes, skinned
3 green chillies
1 cup coriander leaves
7 black pepper corns
1½ tsp. cumin seeds, broiled
1½ tsp. coriander seeds,
   broiled
1" fresh turmeric
5 dried Kashmiri chillies
8 large cloves garlic
2 sprigs curry leaves
Salt
Sesame oil

Grind fine with a little water

Preparation time	:	15 mins.
Cooking time	:	22-25 mins.
Serves	:	4-6

- Salt the prawns and set aside.

- Cook the onions in 3 tablespoons of sesame oil in a pan over a medium flame till soft and pink. Add the salted prawns and the ground masala and cook for 5 minutes and then add the tomatoes and cut vegetable. Stir and cover with a lid. Add water to the lid and turn the fire very low. Cook till the prawns are soft and almost all the vegetable juice has evaporated.

- Serve with rice or rotlis, date and sweet mango chutney.

KHICHRI-MA-KOLMI

(Khichri cooked with Prawns)

For the Rice:

400 gms. basmati rice
1 tsp. haldi
5 black peppercorns
2 star anise
2 deep fried onions
Salt
Pure Ghee

For the Prawn Masala:

250-300 gms. fresh, shelled,
    deveined and washed medium
    sized prawns
½ grated coconut ⎤
6 green chillies, deseeded   Grind
    and chopped   fine
1 tsp. broiled cumin seeds   with
1 tsp. broiled coriander seeds   a little
1 tsp. broiled fennel seeds ⎦ water
Salt
Pure ghee

To add to the cooked rice:

4 boiled eggs, each cut into 2
2 sour limes juice + 2 tbsps. sugar

Preparation time	:	20 mins.
Cooking time	:	45-50 mins.
Serves	:	4-6

- Wash the prawns, salt them and set aside.

- Wash the rice and cook them in a rice cooker along with haldi, black peppercorns, star anise, fried onions, salt and 1 tbsp. of ghee.

- Place the prawns, masala and 2 tbsps. ghee in a vessel and mix well. Heat over a low fire for 5 minutes. Add 1½ cups of water and allow to simmer till amost dry.

- Place the cooked khichri in a thali. Mix in the prawns and sprinkle over with the lime juice and sugar mixture.

- Place in a clean vessel and decorate with boiled eggs. Seal with a tight lid.

- Heat over a tava on a medium heat for 20 minutes.

- Serve with kachumber, papads and a mewa-ne-keri-nu-achaar.

KOLMI-NE-PAPRI-NA-BEEJ-KHATTA-MITHA

(Sweet and sour Prawns and Papri Beans)

350 gms. shelled, deveined, washed
   prawns
400 gms. fresh papri seeds
200 gms. onions, finely chopped
5 large tomatoes, skinned
   and chopped
½ fresh coconut, grated
½ cup peanuts
8 green chillies, deseeded
1 cup fresh coriander leaves,   } Grind
   chopped   fine
15 black peppercorns
3 green cardamoms, seeds
   only
1 star anise
1 tsp. shahjeera
1 flower mace
1½ cups chowlai bhaji
   leaves
2 sprigs curry leaves
Salt
Sesame oil

Preparation time	:	15 mins.
Cooking time	:	45-50 mins.
Serves	:	4-6

- Cook the papri seeds with a little salt in the pressure cooker. They should be intact and not pulpy.

- Place the chopped onions in a vessel along with 3 tablespoons of ghee and the curry sprigs. Cook the onions till soft and add the masala and stir it and fry it for 5 minutes on a low flame. Add the washed prawns after salting them and cover and cook for 5 minutes. Add the chopped chowlai and tomatoes and simmer for 10 minutes. Then add the papri beans and any water that has remained and simmer till the prawns and seeds are almost dry. Taste for salt.

- Serve with vegetable cutlets and wheat flour rotlis.

BHAJI-MA-KOLMI

(Prawns cooked in Spinach)

400 gms. prawns, shelled, deveined
    and washed
3 bunches of chowlai bhaji leaves
    thoroughly washed and cut very
    fine along with very tender
    stems
2 bunches of palak bhaji, only leaves
4 onions, deep fried, and ground on
    a stone pestle
6 green chillies, deseeded   ⎤ Grind
10 black peppercorns   ⎥ fine
4 green cardamoms,   ⎥ with a
    seeds only   ⎬ little
1½" ginger   ⎥ water
1 star anise   ⎦
1 tsp. mustard powder
1 cup thick cream
1 tsp. sour lime juice
Salt
Saltless white butter or
Pure ghee

Preparation time	:	15 mins.
Cooking time	:	45 mins.
Serves	:	4-6

- Place the crushed onions in a vessel and add the ground masala along with the prawns and some salt. Stir for 3 to 5 minutes and then add the chopped chowlai and palak bhaji. Cook over a low fire till you obtain a soft pulpy spinach. Taste for salt.

- Mash the soft cooked spinach with a large spoon and dry up the water.

- Squeeze the sour lime over the bhaji and mix well.

- Serve hot with yellow toover dal with vaghar and rice or wheat rotlis.

NARGOLWALI-KOLMI

(Prawns Nargol Style)

15 very large prawns, with head cut upto the eyes, shelled, deveined, washed twice
7 green chillies, cut julienne
1 tbsp. fresh ginger, sliced, cut julienne
1 tbsp. garlic, sliced, cut julienne
6 sprig onions, cut thickly julienne upto 6" from the root
1 raw mango, peeled, cut into half and sliced julienne
½ tsp. mustard seeds
1 tbsp. fennel seeds, broiled
1 tsp. cumin seeds, broiled
2 tbsps. rice flour
2 sprigs curry leaves
Salt
Sesame oil

Preparation time	:	14 mins.
Cooking time	:	20-25 mins.
Serves	:	4-6

- Salt the prawns and put them in a cool place.

- Heat 2 tablespoons of sesame oil in a langri. When very hot, add the mustard, fennel, cumin seeds and the curry leaves and immediately lower the flame. Mix for 2 minutes and add the green chillies, ginger, garlic and spring onions and allow to cook for 3 more minutes before adding the prawns.

- Allow the prawns to cook in their own juice for 5 minutes, stirring gently all the time.

- Mix the rice flour with 1½ cups of water. Mix well and add to the prawns. Add the mango. Keep stirring non-stop for 5 minutes and when the flour has amalgamated with the water, allow to simmer for 10 more minutes. Taste for salt.

- When the prawns have become soft, remove from the fire.

- Serve with white rice and papads.

LEVTA (MUD FISH)-NO-SANDOVELO-PATIO

500 gms. mud fish, large ones or
   baby ones
250 gms. onions
4 green chillies, deseeded
4 Kashmiri chillies, deseeded
1 large bulb garlic
1 tbsp. cumin seeds
1 tsp. turmeric powder
1 tbsp. Parsi dhansakh masala
1 tsp. black pepper powder
1 bunch fresh coriander,
   finely chopped and ground
½ cup tamarind pulp
1 cup rice flour
Salt
Sesame oil

> Grind well with a little water

Preparation time	:	25-30 mins.
Cooking time	:	20 mins.
Serves	:	4-6

- Wash the mudfish, apply a little salt and set it aside for 20 minutes. Then, add the rice flour and scrub the mud fish and wash it twice so they lose all their scales.

- Slice the onion and set aside.

- Place the mud fish in a vessel and add 3 tablespoons of oil and mix both items well and allow to marinade for 30 minutes.

- Place a karahi with 2 cups of oil on a medium flame and deep fry the onions till golden brown. Drain the onions in a sieve.

- Add the fried onions and ground masala to the marinated mud fish along with a little salt and cook in the tamarind pulp over a low fire without water till soft.

KOLMI-NO-SADO-PULAO

(Simple Prawn Pulao)

850 gms. rice, boiled and drained
650 gms. medium-sized prawns,
   shelled, deveined, washed twice
3 finely chopped onions
1½ tbsp. cumin seeds
10 large cloves garlic⎤ Grind fine
10 green chillies, ⎬ in a little
   deseeded ⎦ water
6 spring onions, cut julienne
4 slices ginger, cut julienne
½ cup boiled green peas
1½ cups potatoes, cubed and deep
   fried
2 onions, sliced and deep fried
6 boiled eggs, each cut into 2
Juice of 3 sour limes + 3 tsps.
   sugar, mixed
Salt
Ghee

Preparation time	:	15 mins.
Cooking time	:	35 mins.
Serves	:	6-8

- Place 2 tablespoons of pure ghee in a large langri and put it on a medium flame. When the oil gets hot, add the ground cumin, garlic and chillies, and lower the heat. Cook for 2 minutes and add the prawns and cover and cook the prawns in their own juice for 5 to 7 minutes. Add a little water at a time and cook till the prawns are soft.

- Take a karahi, add 2 tablespoons of ghee and heat over a low flame. Add the spring onions and finely cut ginger and cook for 3 minutes. Add the boiled green peas and the fried potato cubes as well as the cooked prawns to the rice. Mix well and add the lime juice mixed with sugar. Mix well and arrange the eggs on top of the rice. Cover tightly with foil and place for 10 minutes over a hot tava placed on medium heat.

- Serve with a kachumber and sweet mango chutney.

TAMBOTAN-NA-RAS-MA-KOLMI

(Prawns in Tomato Gravy)

1 kg. tomatoes, skinned and pureed
1 kg. shelled, deveined prawns
3 large onions, chopped fine
½ cup thick coconut juice
½ cup chopped fresh coriander
3 green chillies, slit and deseeded
8-10 Kashmiri chillies ⎤
1½ fresh ginger ⎟
1 tbsp. broiled cumin seeds ⎬ Grind
1 tbsp. broiled coriander seeds ⎟ fine
1 tbsp. broiled fennel seeds ⎦
2 all spice leaves or 2 dried Bay
  leaves
1 golden pepper, cut in strips
1 green pepper, cut in strips
6 large mint leaves
2 tsps. sugar
2 sprigs curry leaves
Salt
Sesame oil

Preparation time	:	20 mins.
Cooking time	:	35 mins.
Serves	:	6-8

- Grind the masala till very soft.

- Place the chopped onions in a vessel with 3 tablespoons of oil and the curry sprigs and bay leaves over a medium flame. Cook till soft and pink.

- Lower the flame and add the ground masala and stir for 5 minutes until it is cooked and becomes red hot. Then add the salted prawns and stir them for 5 minutes. Add the coconut milk, cook the prawns for 3 minutes and then add the tomato puree and salt and allow to simmer for 10 minutes over a low flame. Remove from the fire. Add lightly fried pepper strips.

- Serve over a dish of green peas rice cooked with Star Anise and green cardamoms. Decorate the rice with diamond shapes cut from golden and red peppers.

- Sprinkle the prawns with chopped coriander and the mint leaves.

MALAI-MA-RAMAS-NU-ISTOO

(Ramas Fish Stew)

1 gm. saffron
300 ml. cream
1 medium sized ramas, cut
  into 12 skinless
2" × 2" fillets. Retain skin
  and bones
3 baby carrots, cut into slices
  and boiled
20 baby potatoes, boiled, skinned
  and deep fried
20 baby onions, deep fried
6-8 green chillies, deseeded and
  finely chopped
2 tbsps. chopped parsley
6 3" pieces of celery stalks
2 fresh or dried all-spice leaves or
  bay leaves
2 tbsps. pickled green peppercorns
8 baby tomatoes
3 sprigs dill
Salt
Yellow butter

Preparation time	:	18 mins.
Cooking time	:	30-35 mins.
Serves	:	6-8

- First, make the fish soup by washing the skin and bones twice. Then boil them in a large pan along with 4 cups of water, 1 coarsely chopped onion, 1 chopped large tomato, 3 celery leaves, 5 black peppercorns, and 1" piece crushed ginger. Add a little salt and boil until only 2 cups of soup remains. Strain through a fine sieve into a clean vessel.

- Wash the fillets twice. Place them in the soup and cook them over a medium flame along with the green chillies and the parsley.

- Add 2 tablespoons of butter, allow it to melt and thicken the soup. Mix the cream and stir it into the fish soup.

- Keep over a low flame till the cream is mixed well.

- Heat the saffron till crisp and crush it over the fish. Remove from the fire.

- When ready to eat, reheat the fish over a low fire. Warm the vegetables.

- Place the fish and cream sauce into a shallow dish and top with the vegetables.

- Serve with bread slices and a sweet mongo or carrot chutney.

Chicken

Whenever we had guests at Tadgaon, it was my great grandfather Bawaji's turn to slaughter the chickens. He would wash his face and hands, and do his kusti. Then he would pluck some feathers from each chicken's neck and then cut the throat with his pen knife and throw the bird on the patch of ash in front of the Sarbati Limboo tree in Maiji's backyard.

The Limboo tree gave large green limes. They had orange-yellow flesh and were wonderful for making drinks with sugar and cold water. During its fruiting season, it used to be covered with limboos. I remember eating even the skin, as a child, with my dhansakh.

Once the chickens stopped fluttering, a large vessel of boiling water was brought out and Diwali and Mani, the maidservants, plucked and washed them.

They were cut in a different manner than what I use today. Two large cuts were placed at the neck and shoulder portion and the fingers of both hands were placed inside the cuts. Then, the chicken was torn apart into two equal parts. This method was good and convenient because the stomach was kept whole and was full of wonderful egg yolks. This stomach portion was called the "thatha" and everyone looked forward to eating it.

Being free range chickens, eating good grain, insects and always foraging for worms in the grass, the flesh had a delicious taste, totally unlike the tasteless broilers that are in the market today. The chickens were quality birds indeed.

Once, during the tail end of our May vacation, the day before we left, Maiji had requested Bawaji for 4 large hens to be turned into "Bhatiyu" for us to take to Bombay. One of the hens "Thatha" revealed a perfect egg, ready to be laid the next morning as well as yolks in various stages. Maiji immediately fried the egg and gave it to me to eat at once.

I have never eaten such a delicious chicken as Soonamai's "bhatiya-ni-marghi". It was packed along with chunks of fried potatoes in "Patraval" – a plate made from 8 to 10 dried leaves all sewn together with natural tree bark and made into a large plate.

① Mango and Dried Fruit Chutney (1)
② Chicken Mince with Almonds and Raisins (2)
③ ④ Aléti - Paléti (Chicken Livers and Gizzards) (3)
Brains Cooked in Garlic (4)

VATANA-PAPETA-NI-MARGHI

(Chicken Cooked with Green Peas)

1 Chicken cut into 2 legs and
   2 breasts and then each piece cut
   into 2 again
400 gms. shelled green peas
3 large potatoes, skinned and cut
   into 1" pieces
300 gms. onions, chopped
½ tsp. mustard seeds
1 tsp. turmeric powder
6 Kashmiri chillies
8 large cloves garlic
¼ piece of kopra   Grind fine
7 black peppercorns   with a little
3 green cardamoms,   water
   seeds only
½ tsp. aniseeds
Salt
Sunflower oil

Preparation time	:	12 mins.
Cooking time	:	1 hr.
Serves	:	5

- Wash the chicken twice, cut it into 8 pieces, salt it and set aside.

- Place the chopped onions in a large pan along with 3 tablespoons oil and cook till soft. Then add the mustard seeds, cook for 2 minutes and add the turmeric powder, ground masala and cook for 7 minutes. Then add the tomatoes, potatoes and washed green peas, stir for 3 minutes and add 3 cups of water, cover and allow to simmer till the chicken and peas are tender. Taste for salt.

- Place water on the lid and keep pouring it into the chicken, as required.

- Serve with rice or wheat rotlis and a tomato chutney.

Mutton with Papaya (1)
Kababs with Papri (2)
Chicken Farcha Cooked
with Green Chilli Masala (3)

MARGHI-NA-TUKRA-NU-ACHAAR
(Boneless Chicken Pickle)

12 deboned chicken breasts, each
   cut into 3 pieces, washed twice
1½ tbsp. ground ginger-garlic paste
16 red chillies ⎤
½ tbsp. turmeric powder ⎥ Grind
1½ tbsps. black pepper, clove ⎥ in a
   and cinnamon powder ⎬ little
1 tsp. coriander seeds ⎥ vinegar
1 tsp. cardamom seeds ⎥
Vinegar ⎦
Salt
Sesame Oil

Preparation time	:	15 mins.
Cooking time	:	1 hour
Serves	:	8

- Place the washed pieces of chicken in a vessel. Marinade it in salt, ginger-garlic paste, ground chilli masala, turmeric and the garam masala. Set aside for 2 hours.

- Take a large patia and pour in 1 teacup oil. Allow it to heat and add the chicken pieces and fry the chicken over a slow fire for 7 minutes. If necessary, add more oil.

- Reduce the heat to very low and add 3 cups of vinegar. Mix well and cover. Simmer until the chicken is tender and soft. Taste for salt.

- Remove from the fire and cool.

- Seal tightly in a large glass bottle.

- Ideal to be taken on picnics and whilst traveling.

ALÉTI-PALÉTI
(Fried Chicken Livers and Gizzards)

350 gms. chicken livers
100 gms. chicken gizzards
2 onions, skinned, halved
   and finely sliced
1 tbsp. minced ginger
¾ tsp. turmeric powder
1 tsp. chilli powder
1½ tsps. garam masala
10 curry leaves
Salt
Ghee
2 tbsps. vinegar + 2 tbsps. sugar
   (optional)

Preparation time	:	10 mins.
Cooking time	:	30-35 mins.
Serves	:	4

- Wash the livers and slice and wash the gizzards. Salt them.

- Cook the gizzards in 2 cups of water in the pressure cooker till soft.

- Place a karahi or frying pan on a medium fire with 2 tablespoons of pure ghee. Crush the sliced onions and add them to it along with the curry leaves and minced ginger. Lower the flame and allow to fry till crisp. Add the turmeric, chilli and garam masala.

- Add the chicken livers and drained gizzards and stir-fry for 7 minutes. If you like, you can put in vinegar and sugar and remove from the fire after 2 minutes.

- Serve as a breakfast dish.

BHUNJELI-AAKHI-MARGHI
(Roasted Whole Chicken)

1 large chicken of 1200 gms.

Juice of 1 sour lime ⎤ For washing
Little rice or wheat flour ⎦ the bird

For the Marinade:

3 tbsps. ginger juice
1 tbsp. black pepper powder
Salt

For the Stuffing:

30 gms. ground almonds
1 large onion, finely chopped
200 gms. minced mutton
2 stalks celery, chopped fine
2 apples, skinned, cored and
    chopped into ½" squares
½ tsp. chilli powder
½ tsp. garam masala
1 large pinch mace powder
Salt
White butter, unsalted or
    pure ghee

For the Decoration:

6 large potatoes, cut into halves,
    salted and fried

Preparation time	:	15 mins.
Cooking time	:	1 hr. 15 mins.
Serves	:	4-6

- Cut off the neck of the chicken. Clean it well. It should be thoroughly washed, inside and outside, with rice or wheat flour and sour lime juice. All the stomach remains must be cleaned up.
- Marinade the chicken in salt, pepper powder and the ginger juice for 2 hours.
- To cook the stuffing, chop the onion fine and place in a flat-bottomed vessel with 2 tablespoons of butter and cook over a low heat till soft. Apply the ginger-garlic paste and salt to the mince and add it to the onions and stir gently.
- Lower the flame and add the crisped saffron, chopped celery, almonds, apples, chilli powder, garam masala and mace. Mix well and add a cup of water and allow to simmer till soft, tender and dry. Add more water if necessary. Taste for salt.
- Cool the mince and stuff it into the bird's cavity.
- Take a white cord, insert it into a large needle and stitch up both the bird's extremities. Tie the legs together.
- Place ½ cup of pure ghee in a large karahi and allow it to heat well. Then place the chicken into it and fry it to a red brown colour. Remove from the fire.
- Place it in an oven with 1 cup of water, at 350°F or in a large vessel with water and simmer for 1 hour.
- Keep basting the chicken, every now and then. Add more water as necessary. Cook until the bird is soft and tender.
- Fry the halved potatoes to a golden colour.
- Place the chicken onto a flat dish or salver. Surround it with the halved potatoes and pour any left over gravy onto them.
- Serve warm with a peach salad and buttered bread rolls.

MARGHI-NI-MULAKDANI
(Chicken Mulakdani)

1 gm. saffron
1500 gms. breast and leg pieces of
   chicken
700 gms. leg mutton chunks
2 large onions, finely chopped
1 fresh coconut grated
6 green chillies
1½ tbsps. ginger-garlic paste
3 tbsps. poppy seeds
1 tbsp. cumin seeds
1 tbsp. coriander seeds, broiled
1 tbsp. black peppercorns
1 2" piece cinnamon
5 cloves
4 green cardamom seeds only
1 tsp. turmeric powder
15-18 almonds
Salt
Pure ghee

- Wash the chicken pieces twice and marinade it in the salt and ginger-garlic paste.
- Place the finely chopped onions in a tapeli along with 2 tablespoons of ghee and place on a medium heat. Allow the onions to turn light brown and then add the chicken pieces. Mix well till the chicken pieces turn red-brown and then add 4 cups of water and allow the chicken to cook till soft and only about 1 cup of soup remains. Remove from the fire and set aside.
- Place the mutton, after washing it twice, in a pressure cooker. Add salt and 4 cups of water and allow the mutton to cook till tender and only 2 cups of soup are left. Remove from the fire and strain the soup through a fine sieve into a large tapeli.
- Grind together ½ a grated coconut, green chillies, cumin, coriander and poppy seeds, black peppercorns, turmeric, cinnamon, cloves and cardamom seeds to a very fine paste with the help of ½ cup of water.
- Boil the almonds, skin them, and grind fine.
- Remove thick milk from the remaining half of the grated coconut.
- Place the tapeli with the mutton soup on a low flame and add the ground masala to it and stir for 5 minutes. Then add the cooked chicken pieces along with the soup and allow to simmer for 5 minutes.
- Add the coconut milk and ground almonds to the chicken in the tapeli and stir gently. Taste for salt.
- Also add the saffron after making it crisp on an iron tava and mixing it in the lime juice. Remove chicken from the fire within 5 minutes.
- Serve with parathas and green vegetables cooked in a cheesy sauce or serve with a peas pulao or vegetable khichri.

Preparation time	:	20 mins.
Cooking time	:	45-50 mins.
Serves	:	6-8

BADAM-KISMIS-NA-MASALA-MA-MARGHI

(Chicken cooked in Almond and Raisin masala)

1 whole chicken, cut into 8 pieces
  and washed and salted
3 medium sized onions,
  finely chopped
100 gms. almonds,
  boiled and peeled
125 gms. washed,
  seedless raisins
6 Kashmiri chillies,
  deseeded
½" piece cinnamon
6 black peppercorns
½ tsp. shahjeera
2 cloves
½ tsp. crushed javintri
½" fresh ginger
6 large garlic cloves
½ star anise
6 potatoes, skinned and cut into
  1" cubes
Salt
Pure ghee

Grind
fine in
a little
water

Preparation time	:	15-20 mins.
Cooking time	:	35-45 mins.
Serves	:	6

- Take a flat-bottomed vessel, add 3 tablespoons of ghee and cook the onions till soft and brown. Then add the chicken and brown it over a low fire for 5 to 7 minutes. Then add the ground masala including the clean water from the mixie or stone used for washing it. Cover and keep for 10 minutes, turning the pieces over several times.

- Add 3 cups of water and cook on simmer till the chicken is tender.

- Deep fry the potatoes after soaking them in salted water for ½ an hour. Cook till soft and golden brown. Remove from the karahi and straight away add them to the chicken gravy.

- Serve hot with rotis and a pineapple-onion kachumber.

LEELA MARCHAN-MA-RANDHELA-FARCHA

(Fried Chicken cooked in Green Chillies)

1 chicken, cut into 8 pieces
6-8 green chillies, deseeded ⎤ Grind
1" amba harad or fresh ginger ⎥ fine in
6 black peppercorns ⎥ the
1 tsp. broiled cumin ⎥ juice
1 tsp. turmeric powder ⎥ of 3-4
½ cup fresh coriander, ⎥ sour
   finely chopped ⎦ limes
3 eggs
Breadcrumbs
Salt
Refined oil

Preparation time	:	20 mins.
Cooking time	:	20-25 mins.
Serves	:	6

- Wash the chicken pieces well and marinate them in the ground masala and salt. Smear the masala well and add every drop of lime juice. Keep for 2 hours.

- Cook the chicken pieces in half a litre of hot boiling water. Cover and reduce the heat and cook till the gravy has dried up.

- Roll the chicken pieces in the breadcrumbs.

- Beat the eggs well.

- Heat a karahi half-filled with oil. When it boils, lower the flame a little and dip the chicken pieces in the egg and put them in the oil and allow to cook till golden brown.

- Serve along with fingerchips and a green salad.

MARGHI-MALAI-MA-RANDHELI

(Chicken cooked in Cream)

1 chicken, cut into 8 pieces
    (2 full legs and 2 full breasts,
    each cut into 2 pieces)
2 leaves Allspice
2 tbsps. ginger juice
2 tsps. pepper
200 gms. thick cream
2 stalks of celery, cut into
    2" pieces each
Salt
Pure ghee or Butter

Preparation time	:	2 hrs. for marinating
Cooking time	:	35-40 mins.
Serves	:	4-6

- Wash the chicken twice and marinade in salt, black pepper powder and ginger juice for 2 hours.

- Heat 3 tablespoons ghee or butter in a large pan over a medium flame. When hot, place the chicken in the hot ghee and cook till both sides are red. Then pour in 4 cups of water and put in the celery and cook the chicken till tender. At least 2 to 1½ cups of gravy should remain in the pan. Taste for salt.

- Lower the flame, gently whisk the cream with a pinch of salt and add it to the pan. Mix gently. Simmer for 10 minutes before removing from the fire.

- Serve with mashed potatoes, boiled carrots, creamed beetroots, sweet and sour mango pickle and French Bread or gutlis from your local bakery.

BADAM-DARAKH-NO-MARGHI-NO-KHEEMO
(Chicken Mince with Almonds & Raisins)

750 gms. chicken mince
200 gms. onions, finely chopped
2 cups fresh tomato purée
1 tbsp. minceed ginger
⅓ cup finely chopped coriander
5 green chillies, deseeded, finely
   chopped
5 Kashmiri chillies ⎤
1 star anise |
5 black peppercorns | Broil and
1" piece cinnamon | dry grind
2 cloves | to a
¼ tsp. caraway seeds | powder
½ tsp. shahjeera seeds |
2 mace flowers (javintri) ⎦
150 gms. almonds, boiled, skinned,
   sliced
150 gms. raisins, washed
Salt
Pure Ghee

Preparation time	:	12 mins.
Cooking time	:	30-35 mins.
Serves	:	6-8

• Place a karahi with ½ cup pure ghee on a medium flame. When hot, lower the heat and gently fry the almonds slices to a golden colour and remove from the heat. Fry the raisins in the same ghee and remove and set aside.

• Place the leftover ghee from the karahi into a tapeli, put in the onions and ginger and fry to a light brown colour. Add the mince and some salt and lower the flame and cook for 7 minutes, stirring all the time. Then add the powdered masala, green chillies and the coriander and stir for 3 minutes. Add 2 cups of water, raise the heat, and bring to a boil. Taste for salt.

• When the water begins to dry up, add the fresh tomato purée and cook till the mince is soft and tender.

• Place the mince into a dish whilst hot and cover with the fried almonds and raisins.

• Serve with hot parathas or a vegetable khichdi or a peas pulao.

MARGHI-NA-KHEEMA-NA-BHARELA-KAVAB

(Stuffed Chicken Balls)

500 gms freshly ground
   chicken – no skin
   should be used
1 medium onion, finely
   chopped
1½ tsps. red chilli powder   } Mix in
2½ tsps. dhansakh masala   a thali
1 tsp. turmeric power
2 tbsps. finely chopped
   fresh coriander
1 tbsp. ginger-garlic paste

For the Stuffing:

6 boiled egg yolks
1 onion, finely chopped
   and fried
4 green chillies, deseeded   } Mix
¼ tsp. black pepper powder   well
⅓ piece of sour lime for juice
Salt
4-6 eggs
Breadcrumbs
Salt
Refined Oil

Preparation time	:	25-30 mins.
Cooking time	:	20 mins.
Serves	:	6

- Mix all the mince and the other items in a thali. Beat one egg and add it to the mixture to make it sticky.

- Make balls, slightly larger than a sour lime. Place ¾ teaspoon of the boiled egg yolk mixture into a cup made from the mince, and with hands form into a circular ball.

- When all the stuffing has been used up, roll the chicken balls in the breadcrumbs.

- Whip the eggs.

- Heat ½ a karahi of oil. When hot, dip each chicken ball into the whisked eggs. Carefully put 5 or 6 of them at a time in the hot oil. Fry till golden brown.

- Serve hot as snacks.

MARGHI-NA-KHEEMA-NA-PATTICE
(Minced Chicken Patties)

500 gms. mashed potatoes
2 tbsps. finely chopped fresh
   coriander
½ tsp. black pepper powder
Salt
5 raw chicken breasts, minced
1 onion, finely chopped
6 green chillies, deseeded and
   chopped fine
1½ tsp. finely chopped ginger and
   garlic
1 tsp. garam masala
½ tsp. red chilli powder
½ tsp. turmeric powder
¼ cup vinegar
¼ cup sugar
Salt
¼ cup raisins
¼ cup boiled, skinned, chopped
   almonds
4-6 eggs
Breadcrumbs
Refined oil

Preparation time	:	25 mins.
Cooking time	:	40 mins.
Serves	:	6-10

- Cook the onions in 2 tablespoons of oil till soft and pink in a large vessel. Add the chopped ginger-garlic, the green chillies and the garam masala, chilli and turmeric powders. Mix well for 3 minutes and then add the chicken mince. Lower the flame and allow to cook in its own juice. If necessary, add some more water from time to time.

- When the mince is soft and tender, wash the raisins and add them along with the chopped almonds to the mince. Stir for 2 minutes and then add the vinegar and sugar. Cook till dry. Remove from fire.

- Place the mashed potatoes, salt and pepper in a thali and mix well till soft. Sprinkle the chopped coriander over the potatoes and mix well again. Make 10 to 12 balls out of the potatoes.

- Grease your hands with oil and place one potato ball in your left palm and pat it out into a circle. Place 1 tablespoon of the cooked chicken mince in the center of the potato circle and cover the mince up into a pattice. After you have stuffed all the potato balls, place a karahi half full of oil on a medium flame.

- Whisk the eggs.

- Spread the crumbs on a wooden board. One by one cover all the patties in the crumbs.

- When the oil becomes very hot, lower the flame a little and dip the pattice into the whisked eggs. Then, gently lower each into the hot oil. Fry in batches of 3 at a time till golden coloured.

- Serve with a green salad with rings of spring onions and beetroots.

KATY DALAL'S CHICKEN & RAISIN SAMOSAS

For the Covering:

250 gms maida or self-raising flour
15 gms ghee
½ tsp. salt
½ tsp. cumin
¾ cup water

For the Chicken Mince:

200 gms. chicken mince
1½ medium onions, minced fine
½ tsp. chilli powder
¼ tsp. turmeric powder
1½ tsp. ginger-garlic paste
50 gms. seedless raisins
50 gms. charoli
100 gms. sugar
½ teacup vinegar
¼ cup chopped coriander leaves
½ tsp. salt
Oil

Preparation time	:	10 mins.
Cooking time	:	25-30 mins.
Makes	:	12

- Mix the flour, ghee, salt and cumin and gradually add the water and knead for 10 minutes into a smooth dough. Form into a ball, cover with a damp cloth and keep aside for 30 minutes.

- Mix the chicken mince, ginger-garlic paste and salt.

- Heat a vessel with 2 tablespoons of oil and cook onions over a medium flame till soft and pink and then add the turmeric and chilli powders and the chicken mince and fry over a low heat for 7 minutes. The mince will release its own water. Add the vinegar and sugar and chopped coriander. Mix well and cook till the mince is tender. This should take 10 to 12 minutes.

- Wash the raisins. Fry in a small saucepan along with the charoli and add it to the mince.

- Make the flour into along thick roll and cut into 6 pieces. Take one piece and roll it into a saucer sized chapatti. Cut into 2 half circles.

- Pick up one piece and place it on the palm of your left hand. Dampen the straight side, then join the 2 sides into a cone and press, so the cone is joined. Then stuff it with mince. Again dampen both sides which rise above the stuffing and join them to form a triangle by pressing each corner into the opposite side. Press the bottom so the samoosa can stand up.

- Heat ½ a karahi of oil and when hot, fry 4 samosas at a time till golden red. Remove and place in a colander.

- Serve with sweet date and tamarind chutney or green coconut chutney.

KHARA-TARELA-PAPETA-NI-MARGHI

(Plain Chicken with Fried Potatoes)

1 kg. chicken, cut into 8 pieces
6 medium sized potatoes, skinned
   and cut into halves
2 large onions, finely chopped
4 green chillies, deseeded and slit
1 tsp. ginger-garlic paste
3 bayleaves
5 black peppercorns
1 star anise
1 clove
½" piece cinnamon
Salt
Ghee/oil

Preparation time	:	12 mins.
Cooking time	:	35-40 mins.
Serves	:	4-6

- Wash the chicken twice and apply salt and ginger-garlic paste and set aside.

- Chop the onion and place in a tapeli with 3 tablespoons of ghee. Cook till soft and pink and then put in the bayleaves, peppercorns, star anise, clove and cinnamon and allow to fry for 5 minutes.

- When the whole spice turns red, add the chicken pieces, mix gently, cover and cook in its own juice for 7 minutes over a low flame. Add 3 cups of water and simmer till tender.

- Half fill a karahi with oil. Place on medium heat till hot. Drain the potatoes and fry in 2 batches till golden red.

- When the chicken is tender, taste for salt.

- Uncover and add the potatoes and simmer for a further 7 minutes.

- Serve with bread slices and a tomato chutney.

KESAR-NE-DAHI-MA-MARGHI

(Chicken cooked in Saffron and Curds)

1 1200 gms. chicken
1 teacup whisked curds
1 gm. Saffron
2 large onions, finely chopped
7 Kashmiri chillies, deseeded
1 star anise ⎤
7 black peppercorns │
3 cardamoms, seeds only │ Grind
½" cinnamon piece │ fine
1 tsp. shahjeera ⎬ with a
2" fresh ginger │ little
20 almonds │ water
100 gms. seedless raisins ⎦
¼ cup chopped coriander leaves
Salt
Oil

Preparation time	:	18 mins.
Cooking time	:	45 mins.
Serves	:	4

- Cut the chicken into 2 leg and 2 breast pieces. Then cut each piece into 2 again. Wash them twice, salt them and keep aside.

- Take a large patia and place the onions and 3 tablespoons ghee in it over a medium flame. Cook the onions till golden brown and add the ground masala, stir for 3 minutes and add the chicken. Stir well and allow to cook in its own juice for 7 minutes over a low flame. Add 3 cups of water and cook the chicken on simmer, till soft. Taste for salt and remove from the fire.

- Take the saffron and heat it on an iron tava by pushing it back and forth with a wadded teacloth.

- Replace the tapeli on a slow fire and crumble the saffron onto the chicken and stir and allow it to blend well in the gravy. Whisk the curds and gradually add it to the chicken, along with freshly chopped coriander. Simmer for 10 minutes and remove from the stove.

- Serve with parathas and ground, sweet and savoury palak.

KESAR-NE-DAHI-NI-MARGHI-NO-PULAO

700 gms. basmati rice
5 onions, sliced in half and deep
    fried
1 gm. saffron
2 star anise
15 black peppercorns
2 1" pieces cinnamon
3 cloves
5 green cardamoms, lightly crushed
Salt
Ghee
1 portion of the recipe Kesar-ne-
    Dahi-ma-Marghi
6 large oval-sized potatoes, skinned
    and each cut vertically into
    4 pieces
6 boiled eggs
20 fried whole cashewnuts
40 fried whole raisins
Salt
Ghee

Preparation time	:	10 mins.
Cooking time	:	35-40 mins.
Serves	:	8-10

- Cook the chicken as instructed in the previous page and set aside.

- Place all the contents for the pulao rice into the rice cooker and cook till the grains are tender but separate.

- Boil the eggs.

- Place the cut potatoes into salted water.

- Heat ghee in a karahi and fry the potatoes in batches till golden red.

- Fry the cashew nuts and raisins.

- When it is time to eat, take a large silver salver or flat dish. Arrange the hot chicken pieces and gravy in the center and surround it with the cooked rice and fried potatoes.

- Garnish as seen in the colour plate with sliced eggs and fried cashew nuts and raisins.

- Serve with dhansakh dal and a kachumber and sliced cucumbers, beetroots and green lime pieces.

NARIEL-MA-SADI-MARGHI

(A Simple Chicken Dish cooked in Coconut)

1000 gms. chicken, cut into 2 legs
   and 2 breasts, each cut into
   3 pieces
1 tbsp. ginger pulp
1 coconut, for milk
1 tbsp. cumin seeds
8 large cloves garlic
8-10 green chillies, deseeded   ⎤ Grind
1 tbsp. fennel seeds   ⎬ in
¼ tsp. caraway seeds   water
½ cup chopped coriander
½ cup broken cashew nuts   ⎦
6 potatoes, skinned and sliced
3 bay leaves
4 green cardamom, lightly crushed
Salt
Pure Ghee/Sunflower Oil

Preparation time	:	12-15 mins.
Cooking time	:	35 mins.
Serves	:	4-6

- Take a patia and place 3 tablespoons of ghee in it and put it on medium heat. Wash and salt the chicken pieces.

- When the oil grows hot, add the bay leaves and cardamoms, allow to heat for 2 minutes, add the chicken pieces and allow to brown. Do not scorch them. Mix in the ground masala and lower the flame and allow to cook for 3 minutes, stirring the chicken all the while.

- Add the coconut milk and taste for salt and simmer the chicken till tender.

- Soak the potato slices in salted water.

- Half fill a karahi with oil and place on high heat. When hot, add some of the potato slices and sprinkle a little water on top of the oil and fry till golden red.

- Fry the potato slices in batches, drain and add to the hot chicken gravy.

- Serve with a tomato salad, green beans and bread or rotlis.

JARDALOO-MA-MARGHI

(Chicken cooked with Apricots)

1 chicken, 1200 grms., cut into
    8 pieces. 2 breasts and 2 legs,
    each cut into 2
1 cup curds, whisked along with
    1 gm. of toasted saffron
2 onions, chopped coarsely
10 Kashmiri chillies
2 1" pieces cinnamon
4 cloves   Grind
12 black pepper corns   very fine
1 star anise   with as
4 javintri (mace) flowers   much
1 tbsp. shahjeera   water as
½ cup grated kopra   needed
½ cup broken cashew nuts
15 apricots, soaked overnight in
    water + sugar
4 large tomatoes
Salt
Pure ghee

Preparation time	:	15-20 mins.
Cooking time	:	45 mins.
Serves	:	4-6

- Wash the chicken pieces twice, apply salt and marinade in the whisked curds and saffron.

- Place ½ cup of pure ghee in a large patia, place on medium heat. When the oil heats up, add the finely ground masala and lower the heat. Stir well for 3 to 5 minutes and when the masala becomes red hot, put in the pieces of marinaded chicken. Stir well and cover and allow the chicken to cook in its own juice for 7 minutes. Stir the chicken add 1½ cup of water, cover, place water on the lid and allow to simmer for 15 minutes till tender.

- Add the pulped tomatoes and the apricots drained from the water in which they had been soaked overnight and cook uncovered till the chicken gravy has almost dried up.

- Serve hot with any green vegetables and parathas.

*Eggs with Mawa
and Tomatoes (1)
Apple and Almond
Custard (2)
Chickens Stuffed with
Pulao and Roasted (3)*

BHARELA PARVAL
(Chicken Mince Stuffed Snake Gourd Pieces)

3 tender snake gourds
500 gms. chicken mince
2 large onions, chopped fine
3 tomatoes, skinned and chopped
   fine
$\frac{1}{2}$ cup chopped fresh coriander
1 tsp. turmeric powder
2 tsps. chilli powder
$1\frac{1}{2}$ tsps. Prakash's garam masala
1 tsp. sugar
2 tbsps. charoli
2 tbsps. raisins
3-4 eggs
Breadcrumbs/Bread slices
Salt
Refined Oil

Preparation time	:	15 mins.
Cooking time	:	45 mins.
Serves	:	6-8

- Take a thick string made from coir commonly called "katha" or any abrasive cloth and clean snake gourds of their white skin until only the green skin shows. Wash them. Slice off the ends. Cut the remaining portions into 3" pieces. Remove the soft mush and seeds from the centre until you have a hollow piece like large tube. Wash the pieces and allow to dry.

- Take a vessel, add 2 tablespoons of oil and place it on a medium flame. Add the onions and cook them till they are soft and pink.

- Add the mince with the salt, turmeric, chilli and garam masala and mix well and cook for 5 minutes on a low flame. Then add 1 cup water and cook for a further 10 minutes. Add the tomatoes, raisins and charoli and the coriander and cook till the mince is tender and dry. If necessary, add more water and sugar. Taste for salt and allow the mince to cool.

- Steam or lightly boil the snake gourd pieces in salted water till they are almost cooked. Remove and drain from the water in a sieve.

- Stuff the gourd pieces with the mince.

- Mash 4 slices of the bread in a well-beaten egg in a soup plate. Make tiny nodules and plug the gourd pieces at both ends.

- Place a karahi half-filled with oil on a medium flame. Whisk 2 eggs. When the oil is hot, dip the gourd piece in the beaten eggs and immerse them, a few at a time, and fry them till golden coloured.

- Serve with tomato and papaya gravy.

Boneless Chicken Pickle (1)   ① ②
Mutton Stew (2)   ③
Simple Prawn Pulao (3)

BHUNJELO-MARGHI-NO-KHEEMO
(Baked Chicken Mince)

This is a very delicious dish and must be had as soon as it is cooked. In former times, with no electricity and no pyrex dishes, it was baked in a langri *which was placed upon hot white wooden embers and the lid or top was also covered with white-hot pieces of wood. When the Parsis moved into cities, they used coal. Nowadays, it is a different matter.*

For the Potato Covering:

850 gms. mashed potatoes
6 green chillies, deseeded and cut fine
8 curry leaves, chopped fine
1/2 cup fresh coriander, chopped fine
1 tsp. broiled, crushed, coriander seeds
1" ginger, crushed fine and ground
3 eggs
Salt
Butter

For the Chicken Mince:

750 gms. fine chicken mince
4 apricots, deseeded and chopped finely
100 gms. raisins
50 gms. charoli
1 tbsp. chopped ginger
1 tbsp. chopped garlic
2 tsps. powdered white peppercorns
3 eggs
Salt
Pure Ghee

Preparation time	:	20 mins.
Cooking time	:	50 mins.-1 hour.
Serves	:	6-8

- Grease a baking or pyrex dish with butter.

- Heat 2 teaspoons butter in a small frying pan. When hot, add the green chillies, curry leaves, coriander seeds and ginger. Mix over medium heat for 2 minutes and remove from the fire.

- Place the mashed potatoes onto a thali and add all the fried items to it as well as the freshly chopped coriander leaves. Sprinkle lightly with salt. Add 2 tablespoons of butter and knead the potatoes well. There should be no lumps. Form into a round ball and cover and keep in a cool place till needed.

- Place 3 tablespoons of butter in a large frying pan over medium heat. When the butter liquefies, add the chopped ginger and garlic. Stir fry for 2 minutes and add the apricot pieces, raisins and charoli. Mix for 1 minute and add the mince. Stir over a low fire for 5 minutes. Then add 2 cups of water and keep on simmer until the mince becomes tender and dry. Add salt to taste.

- Separate the yolks and the egg whites.

- Whisk together 3 egg whites and one yolk. Add it to the mashed potato and mix well. Then take the buttered dish. Pat half the potato into the bottom of the vessel and smooth the surface with a spatula.

- Add the mince over the potato into a smooth layer. Press lightly. Then add the remaining half of the potato and smoothen it over the mince.

- Light the oven to 350⁰F

- Whisk the egg yolk and with your fingers, spread it over the potato layer. Bake till golden brown.

- Serve at once with vegetables or masoor dal and green salad.

MAIWAHALAN

(literally means Beloved of the Mother)

1200 gms. whole roast chicken, finely shredded
500 gms. thick cream
8 egg yolks and whites, separated
20 gms. almonds, boiled, sliced and lightly fried
20 gms. pistachios, boiled, sliced and lightly fried
20 gms. seedless raisins, cleaned and lightly fried
10 gms. charoli, washed
1 tsp. minced, deseeded, green chillies
1 large pinch pepper powder
Salt

Preparation time	:	20 mins.
Cooking time	:	20 mins.
Serves	:	6

- Shred the chicken very fine.

- In a thali, gently mix in the chicken, cream, nuts, raisins, minced green chillies, large pinch black pepper powder and a pinch of fine salt.

- Beat the egg whites till stiff and blend into the chicken mixture and transfer it into a rectangular pyrex dish.

- Smoothen the mixture into a flat surface and make 8 depressions into it.

- Take one yolk at a time and place it in each depression. Sprinkle salt lightly on the yolks and place in a hot oven at 350⁰F. Bake for 20 minutes, by which time the eggs should have set.

- Serve straight from the oven with French Bread, butter, lettuce, beetroot, celery and apple salad.

PALAV-BHARELI-BHUNJELI-MARGHI
(Baked Full Chicken Stuffed With Pulao)

3 large chickens, at least
    1200 gms. each

The First Marinade:

Juice of 4 sour limes
2 tsps. aji-no-moto
Salt

The Second Marinade:

12 large deseeded
    Kashmiri chillies
1½" fresh ginger
12 large cloves garlic
20 black peppercorns
1 2" piece cinnamon
1 star anise
4 cloves
¾ cup curds

> Grind very
> fine in
> ½ cup of
> sugarcane
> vinegar

For the Stuffing:

700 gms. basmati rice, cooked
2 cups long cut cooked chicken
    breasts
6 rings canned pineapple, cut into
    ½" pieces
1 tsp. crushed cumin seeds
1 tsp. crushed caraway seeds
2 tsps. crushed black peppercorns
4 tbsps. fried raisins
2 tsps. coarsely ground, sweet dry
    red chilli flakes
6 spring onions, cut juliennes
2 red peppers, cut into star shapes
2 yellow peppers, cut into star
    shapes
Ghee

Preparation time	:	Marinade overnight
Cooking time	:	50 mins.-1 hr.
Serves	:	12

- Wash the 3 chickens inside out. Cut off the legs. Cut the neck 1" above the shoulder.

- Make small cuts on the breats, thighs and drumsticks. Salt the chickens inside out. Mix the lime juice and aji-no-moto and apply it all over the chickens. In case any liquid is left over, apply it into the cavities. Keep in a cool place for 2 hours.

- Grind the masala very fine and place in a glass bowl. Lightly whisk the curds, add salt and mix into the masala bowl. Then apply all over the chickens. Place in a refrigerator, in a covered vessel overnight.

- The next day, take a large flat-bottomed vessel. Add 3 tablespoons ghee to it and place it over a medium heat. When the ghee heats up, add the spring onions, cumin seeds, caraway seeds, black peppercorns, the ground red chilli flakes and the raisins. Lower the heat immediately. Add the cut chicken and mix well. Taste for salt. Allow to heat through for 5 minutes and add the rice and stir gently for 5 minutes. Add the pineapple pieces last of all.

- When the rice becomes cool, stuff it into the chikens' cavities. Stitch the two ends with a needle and a strong white cord or thread.

- You can cook the chickens in an oven at 350⁰F or you can roast them over white-hot coals over which you have placed a *jali*.

- Keep basting the chickens with hot ghee when in an oven or over hot coals. It should take over an hour to cook them well.

- Place over a bed of rice. Decorate with the red and yellow stars cut from the peppers.

- Serve on its own. This dish needs no accompaniments.

duck

OF DUCKS AND DAL-NI-PORIS

Papa's Kakaji Sorabji Frenchman died in 1944 in the Bombay Dock explosion. He left behind 4 daughters, all very loving and clever. Naji was 24 and was working as a teacher, Maki was 22 years old and engaged to Jal, Mehru was 19 and was working in the Red Cross and Roshan, the baby of the family, was only 5 years old.

Kakiji whose name was Jerbai, was a tall, wiry lady. She got up early each morning and first of all, brushed her teeth and did her kusti. Then she made tea for the girls by 7 a.m. as they had to go to work. She had her bath and made a breakfast of milk and bread and butter or a half-boiled egg. Then she would sit down to pray after the 3 elder girls had left for work. Little Roshan joined the St. Joseph's Convent at the age of 6.

I remember Kakiji as always praying in front of a small afarganya *of sukhar and loban. She did loban twice a day, in the mornings and evenings. The diva was lit at night.*

I would be called for a holiday in May by her and when I went home, she would give me a pouch of money with change in it. I remember the old days with much nostalgia and shed a few tears for what has been.

Kakiji's house was opposite the beach and Roshan and I would go right down when the water started coming in and collect a kathli of sea water for sprinkling over the "umbars" in the house. This was especially so in Avan Mahino, which was dedicated to the lady farista Ava Ardavisur Banoo. As I write this, Mehru reminded me that today was Avan Mahino and Avan Roj.

On this day, all Parsis who could make it, went to Apollo Bunder or Chowpatty and did their kusti prayers in front of the ocean because Ardavisur Banoo presided over the waters.

In every Parsi home, dal-ni-pori was made. A sweet mixture of tuvar dal was cooked till it resembled a thick, sticky mass. It was cooked with pure ghee and flavoured with vanilla, cardamom and nutmeg powder and wrapped in a flat maida cake which covered the dal completely. Then, it was rolled into a thick circle by the rolling pin. From each house, at least one pori, along with flowers and a coconut was thrown into the sea.

I remember as a small child on holiday in Tadgaon, going to the beach with Jer Patel and probably her brothers to throw 5 poris which Soonamai had given me to put into the sea.

Even today, most Parsis buy their poris readymade from R.T.I. or friends and eat them without fail on this day.

My friend Dinoo Bhathena would go to Chowpatty for 40 days in a row to pray the Avan Yasht. At the end of it, she would emerge absolutely tanned by an unforgiving sun – her face would be charred black, but this prayer once a year, gave her an immense sense of peace and satisfaction.

A very simple and easy way to make this pori is given in Jamva Chaloji No. 1 on page 33.

Normally, Parsis don't eat much duck flesh. They consider it 'visru' or fishy smelling.

Kakiji lived in Bandra where a lot of Catholic people also lived. Next door to her house, in the same compound, lived several families of poor Catholics, who kept chickens and ducks for sale. So, Kakiji bought her poultry from them. This was very convenient for her as she got very fresh stuff a little cheaper than the market price.

KAKIJINU-GARAM-MASALA-MA-BATAK

(Duck cooked in Garam Masala, Kakiji Style)

1 large duck, cleaned and jointed
3 onions, finely chopped ⎤
2" ginger ⎥ Grind
4 green chillies ⎥ fine
10 cloves of large garlic ⎦
8 red chillies, deseeded ⎤
1 heaped tbsp. garam masala ⎥ Grind
1 tsp. turmeric powder ⎥ fine
1 star anise ⎦
3 large tomatoes, skinned and
   pureed
¼ bunch washed, chopped coriander
2 slit green chillies
Salt
Ghee/Oil

Preparation time	:	20 mins.
Cooking time	:	35 mins.
Serves	:	4-6

- Take one cleaned, jointed, large sized duck. Wash it 2 to 3 times. Salt it very lightly and set aside.

- Grind the onions, ginger, garlic and green chillies very fine and place the masala in a large langri. Add 3 tablespoons ghee or oil and cook it over a low fire. Do not allow it to burn. Cook till the onion sends out a delicious aroma and then add the red chilli masala. Mix well for 3 minutes and then put in the duck pieces. Mix well again and cook for 7 minutes till the pieces are well covered in masala. Add 2 cups of water, stir and cover and cook till soft and dry. Duck is a tougher bird than chicken, so if you need more water, add a little extra at a time. The duck should be tender and the gravy should be dry. Taste for salt after adding water.

- Serve with boiled or golden fried potato halves, and brun pau or peti pau.

112

CHORA-MA-BATAK

(Duck Cooked with Black Eyed Beans)
(A long forgotten recipe)

1 large jointed duck
400 gms. black eyed beans, soaked
    overnight
3 large onions, finely chopped
½ fresh coconut, grated ⎤ Grind fine in
2" cinnamon   water.
                        Reserve the
15 black peppercorns   water which
3 cloves   you use to
8 Kashmiri chillies   rinse the
1 star anise   mixie or
½ tsp. shahjeera   grinding
                       ⎦ stone
1½ tsp. turmeric powder
4 large tomatoes, skinned and
    pureed
Salt
Ghee

Preparation time	:	12-15 mins.
Cooking time	:	50 mins. -1 hr.
Serves	:	6-8

- Soak the black eyed beans overnight.

- Wash the duck pieces 2 to 3 times. Salt them and put them in a cool place for an hour.

- Meanwhile, place the black eyed beans in a pressure cooker with salt and the required water. Upon removal, they should be tender but whole – not mashed up. Cool.

- Place the chopped onions in a large patia. Add 3 tablespoons oil or ghee and cook them until they are light brown. Then add the ground masala and fry it for 3 minutes. Then add the duck pieces and mix well into the masala so that they are well coated with it. Lower the flame and allow the duck to cook in its own juices for 7 minutes. Add the masala water and 2 cups more water and cook till the pieces are soft and tender.

- Open the pressure cooker and add the black eyed beans to the duck pieces along with any left over water in which they were cooked. Stir. Add the fresh tomato puree and allow to simmer for 20 minutes until the bean gravy thickens. Taste for salt. Remove from the fire only when there is no watery content in the patia.

- Serve hot with peti pau, sweet mango pickle and an onion kachumber.

MASALA-NU-BATAK
(Masala Duck)

1 large duck, 1200 gms. cut into
   8 pieces, discard neck and wings
1 tsp. powdered star anise
2 tsps. powdered black peppercorns
1 tbsp. ginger pulp
8 red Goa chillies   ] Grind in
8 large cloves garlic } a little
100 gms. raisins   ] vinegar
2 bay leaves
6 pieces of celery stalks each
   3" long
Salt
Sunflower oil

Preparation time	:	15 mins.
Cooking time	:	35-40 mins.
Serves	:	4-6

- Wash the duck pieces well. Salt the pieces and marinade them in the ginger pulp and the star anise and black peppercorn powders.

- Take a large black karahi and put 3 tablespoons of oil into it and heat it over a medium flame. When hot, add the duck pieces and fry till red. Add the bay leaves and celery pieces and cook for 3 minutes. Lower the flame and add the ground masala and stir fry for 5 minutes. Add a sprinkling of water every few minutes and cook dry till tender.

- Serve with potato chips, lettuce and cucumber salad and French bread or brun pau.

Mutton

In the old days all the Parsi farmers had their own access to fresh mutton. There were shepherds, tall ruddy complexioned men, with handsome acquiline noses and Grecian features who wore huge turbans, a sleeveless undergarment with a sleeveless vest over it, dhotis and huge camel skin joras or pointed-toed boots. The Parsi farmers would give them money to buy kids for them. Then, when the goats grew up, they shared the offspring in money or kind. I have seen these transactions with my own eyes when I was a child. The wily shepherd would always try to beat down the prices and I don't think he ever gave the truthful number of the newborn animals. I once saw one arguing with Cooma, my great-grandfather's niece-in-law, when I was very small.

Later on, when I was in college, I saw my father's sister Khorshed Balsara, doing the same with a shepherd. He had actually brought 4 baby goats to her farmhouse. I picked one up and petted it. It was so cute. Only, half an hour later, I didn't think so. I was covered with huge, red, angry bites of whatever insects were hidden in its sleek, hairy coat.

The Parsi loved his mutton and never considered eating a pure vegetarian meal unless it was one of the 4 days in the month when no meat or chicken was eaten, or it was Bahman Mahino, when flesh was not eaten for an entire month.

Jamva Chaloji No. 1 contains recipes for excellent mutton dishes and pulaos.

AAKHA-TARELA-BHEJA
(Whole Fried Brain)

6 whole sheep's brains
2 tbsps. ginger-garlic and green
    chilli paste
1½ tsps. turmeric powder
½ tsp. red chilli powder
¼ cup chopped coriander leaves
3-4 eggs
Breadcrumbs
Salt
Peanut oil

Preparation time	:	25-30 mins.
Cooking time	:	40 mins.
Serves	:	6

- Soak the brains in water. Add ½ cup of vinegar so that the red skin on top of the brain slips off easily. Wash the brains gently, twice. Apply salt, ginger-garlic-chilli paste, the turmeric and chilli powder and set aside for 30 minutes.

- Take a flat bottomed vessel and place the brains comfortably in it. Sprinkle over the coriander leaves, add ¼ cup water to the pan and gently boil the brains over very low heat.

- Place breadcrumbs on a wooden board. Put oil in a large karahi and place on medium heat. Whisk the eggs in a soup plate.

- Roll each brain gently in the breadcrumbs. See that it is completely coated. When the oil heats up, take one brain at a time and dip it into the hot oil. Reduce heat and allow to fry slowly till golden red. These brains should be served straight from the karahi, piping hot.

- Serve them with fresh brun pau at breakfast.

TAMBOTA-MA-BHEJOO

(Brains Cooked in Tomatoes)

6 sheep's brains
1 kg. tomatoes, skinned and
   chopped
4 large onions, finely chopped
½ cup coriander leaves, finely
   chopped
8 green chillies, deseeded ⎤ Grind
10 large garlic cloves   ⎟ fine
1 tbsp. cumin seeds   ⎬ with a
7 black peppercorns   ⎟ little
25 gms. broken cashewnuts ⎦ water
1½ tsps. turmeric powder
1 tbsp. sugar
Salt
Sunflower oil

Preparation time	:	15 mins.
Cooking time	:	20 mins.
Serves	:	4

- Soak the brains in water along with half a cup of vinegar. This will help to remove the fine red skin over the brain more easily. Wash twice, cut into pieces, marinade in salt the turmeric powder and set aside.

- Place the onions in a vessel which is flat bottomed. Add 3 tablespoons oil and cook till pink and soft. Add the ground masala and cook it for 5 minutes with the onions over a low flame. Add the tomatoes, coriander and sugar and mix well and simmer for 10 minutes till the tomatoes are pulpy. Then take a flat thali-like vessel and put the tomatoes onto it and pat it flat.

- Keep the thali over a low fire and allow the pulp to simmer. Place pieces of the brains onto the flattened pulp and cover and cook. Once gently turn the brains upside down. Cook till the pieces have become firm. Remove from the fire.

- Serve with bread slices or rotlis.

BHAJI-MA-BHEJOO

(Brain Cooked In Spinach or Bhaji)

6 sheep's brains, very fresh
350 gms. onions, halved and
    finely sliced
3 bunches of chowlai bhaji, leaves
    plucked and washed
2 bunches of coriander leaves,
    plucked and washed
8 green chillies, deseeded ⎤ Grind in
10 large cloves of garlic ⎬ a little
1 tbsp. cumin seeds   water
5 black peppercorns   ⎦
1½ tsps. turmeric powder
Salt
Ghee or oil

Preparation time	:	15-20 mins.
Cooking time	:	25 mins.
Serves	:	4-6

- Soak the brains in water with ½ cup of vinegar for 30 minutes. When you clean them, the red thin skin will come off easily. Wash the brains gently and allow the water to drain off. Cut each into 5 pieces. Then marinade in salt and turmeric powder and set aside.

- Wash the chowlai bhaji and the coriander leaves well and chop very finely.

- Place the onions in an open-mouthed vessel along with ½ cup of ghee or oil and fry till golden. Then add the ground masala and cook for 3 minutes till the masala is red. Add the chopped leaves and salt and cook covered over a low fire till they are soft and tender. Mash the cooked bhaji and flatten it out in the bottom of the vessel. Then pick up the marinaded brain pieces and drop them on the top of the smoothened bhaji. Cover and cook till the brains are ready. Shake the vessel from side to side and once very gently, turn them upside down along with the bhaji.

- These are delicious, if had with warm brun pau or ladi pau for breakfast or lunch.

LASAN-MA-BHEJOO

(Brains cooked in Garlic)

6 goat's brains, skinned, cleaned and
    washed twice and each cut into
    4 to 5 pieces
10 large cloves of garlic, peeled and
    crushed
4 onions deep fried in oil
4-6 green chillies, deseeded and
    chopped fine
1 cup finely chopped fresh coriander
1 tsp. garam masala
1 tsp. turmeric powder
½ tsp. red chilli powder
½ tsp. coarsely ground cumin
Salt
Pure ghee

Preparation time	:	15-20 mins.
Cooking time	:	25-30 mins.
Serves	:	5

- Cut and wash the brains, salt them and put them away for ½ hour in a cool place.

- Place 4 teaspoons of ghee in a small flat-bottomed vessel and place on a low flame. Add the crushed garlic and green chillies and cook till the garlic is soft.

- Add the garam masala, turmeric, chilli and cumin powders. Stir and gently add the fried onions and fresh coriander. Mix well for 3 minutes. Do not increase the heat. Take one piece of brain at a time and drop it onto the garlic, onion and coriander mixture. After 5 minutes, turn over the pieces. Cover and cook for 5 minutes more. Remove from the fire and serve as soon as you can.

- Serve with hot rotlis.

Mutton Masala with Kababs (1)
Baked Chicken Mince (2)
Black Lentils with Mutton
and Fried Garlic (3)
Mackerel Curry (4)

TARELA-BAKRA-NA-BHEJA

(Fried Goats' Brains)

4 fresh brains soaked for 30 minutes in a solution of ¼ cup vinegar and 1 cup water
4 green chillies, deseeded and finely chopped
¼ cup chopped fresh coriander
¾ tsp. turmeric powder
½ tsp. black pepper powder
2 tsps. ginger-garlic paste
2 eggs
Breadcrumbs
Salt
Peanut oil

Preparation time	:	20 mins.
Cooking time	:	20 mins.
Serves	:	4-6

- Clean the thin red stringy mush from the brains and wash them well. Check the small triangle at the top of the brain for bones or worms.

- Cut each brain into 2 large pieces and then if necessary, again into 2 pieces. The fifth piece will be the small triangular piece on top of the brain. Apply salt, ginger-garlic paste, the turmeric and black pepper powders and set aside for 30 minutes.

- Place the brain pieces into a thick bottomed pan, sprinkle with the green chillies and coriander and cook in its own juices over a very low fire. Turn once. They should be half cooked in 5 minutes.

- Roll the brain pieces in the breadcrumbs.

- Place half a karahi of oil on a medium flame.

- Whisk 2 eggs in a soup plate. It is possible you may need another one.

- When the oil is hot, dip the breadcrumb covered brain pieces in the eggs and place them in the karahi and fry till golden red.

- Serve with masoor or chana dal and wheat rotlis along with sweet mango chutney.

Tomato Gravy with Papaya (1)
Snake Gourd Pieces Stuffed with Mince (2)
Chicken Farcha in Green Masala (3)

MASALA-NA-KHARIYA
(Trotters in Spicy Gravy)

16 Trotters, front legs each cut into
   3 pieces
500 gms. onions, finely chopped
½ coconut, grated ⎤
8-10 Kashmiri chillies,
   deseeded   Finely
4 green chillies, deseeded   ground
12 black peppercorns   with a
4 cloves   little
1 3" piece cinnamon   water
1 tbsp. cumin
1 cup chopped coriander
   leaves ⎦
2 tsps. turmeric powder
4 tsps. Parsi dhansakh masala
4 tsps. ground ginger-garlic
3 sprigs curry leaves
Salt
Pure ghee

Preparation time	:	10 mins.
Cooking time	:	1 Hr. 30 mins.
Serves	:	8

- Clean the trotters well. Every hair must be well removed. Check for stones between the hooves. Wash at least 3 times before placing them in a pressure cooker along with 3 litres of water, salt, turmeric powder and the ginger-garlic paste. Cook till soft and very tender. If you have more soup than you need, place the trotters in a large pan and boil it so that it gets thicker. Remove from the stove.

- Take a large vessel and cook the onions in ½ to ¾ cup of ghee on a medium flame till soft and of an almond colour. Add the ground masala and fry over a low flame for 7 to 10 minutes, till it is thoroughly cooked. Do not let it burn. If necessary, sprinkle some water and cook till you get a delicious aroma. Then add the cooked trotters and soup and simmer for 15 minutes. Taste for salt. Remove from the fire.

- Serve hot in soup plates along with crisp gutli breads and an onion kachumber and sliced lime pieces.

TATRAVELI-KALEJI-NE-PAPETO

(Sautéed Liver with Potatoes)

1 kg. liver, cleaned and cut into
   1" cubes
500 gms. potatoes, skinned and cut
   into 1" cubes
1½ tsps. turmeric powder
1½ tsps. red chilli powder
1 tsp. black pepper powder
Salt
Peanut oil

Preparation time	:	15 mins.
Cooking time	:	7-8 mins.
Serves	:	6

- Skin the liver, remove the knots and thick white skin inside the liver and cut it into 1" pieces.

- Wash the liver and marinade it in salt, the ginger-garlic paste, and the turmeric, chilli and black pepper powders. Set aside in a cool place.

- Half an hour before you sit down to your meal, skin the potatoes and cut into 1" squares. Soak them in salted water.

- Place a karahi, half filled with oil on a medium flame. When the oil heats up, fry the potatoes in batches till soft and golden in colour. Remove from the fire.

- Take a large frying pan and put in half a cup of oil from the karahi. Heat it and add the liver pieces into the pan and keep the heat low. Shake the pan for 5 to 7 minutes. The liver will be ready to be eaten.

- Remove onto a flat dish and cover with fried potatoes.

- Serve with rotlis and a vegetable.

BOOKKA-NE-TALLI-LAL-MARCHAN-SAATHE

(Kidneys and Spleen with Red Chillies)

5 kidneys, skinned and each cut
    into 2 pieces and cleaned
3 goat's spleens, washed, skinned
    and cut into thick long pieces
4 deseeded Kashmiri chillies
1 tsp. chopped fresh ginger
1½ tsps. crushed garlic
1½ tsps. powdered pepper-cloves-
    cinnamon
8 curry leaves
Salt
Pure ghee

Preparation time	:	5 mins.
Cooking time	:	30-40 mins.
Serves	:	5

- Place the kidneys after salting them in a small metal bowl and pressure cook till tender.

- Salt the spleens and set aside.

- Place the 4 Kashmiri chillies and curry leaves along with 2 tablespoons of ghee in a karahi over a low flame, along with the ginger and garlic. Cook for 3 minutes and add the tender kidneys and spleen pieces and fry well. If necessary, add more ghee. Sprinkle the garam masala and stir well till reddish brown.

- Serve with hot rotlis and scrambled eggs.

DAHI-MA-ANTHELA-CHAAP

(Chops in Curd Sauce)

12 double chops
150 gms. creamy dahi or curds
1½" piece ginger
6 Kashmiri chillies
1 tbsp. coriander seeds   Grind in a little water
1 tbsp. fennel seeds
½ tsp. mace flowers
½ tsp. shahjeera
¼ tsp. caraway seeds
Salt
Pure ghee

Preparation time	:	15-20 mins.
Cooking time	:	40-45 mins.
Serves	:	4-5

- Clean the chops with a damp cloth and beat the flesh with a meat mallet gently, to break down the stringy flesh. Salt them and place them in a neat circle in a thali.

- Apply the ground masala to the chops. Then whisk the curds and apply it to both sides of the chops and allow to marinade for 2 hours.

- Place a very large flat thali on a medium fire with ½ cup of ghee. Allow it to get hot and then arrange the chops in a circle. Lower the heat and cover and cook for 7 minutes. Then turn them over once, cover and cook for 7 more minutes. If you feel that the chops are getting dry, sprinkle 2 tablespoons of water on them. Cook till tender and serve straight from the pan.

MASALA-LAGAARELA-CHAAP

(Chops applied with Masala)

10 double chops
2 tsps. ginger-garlic paste
5 Kashmiri chillies, deseeded ⎤ Grind
7 black peppercorns ⎟ fine
2 cloves ⎟ with a
2 green cardamom seeds ⎬ little
1 tsp. cumin seeds ⎟ water
1 tsp. sesame seeds ⎦
3 eggs
Breadcrumbs
Salt
Pure ghee or Refined oil

Preparation time	:	15 mins.
Cooking time	:	30-35 mins.
Serves	:	5

- Wash the chops, apply salt and the ginger-garlic paste and cook them till tender, along with some water, in a pressure cooker.

- Carefully remove the chops from the cooker and place them on a thali.

- Spread the breadcrumbs on a wooden board.

- Apply the ground paste mixed with a little salt to the chops. Then coat them with the breadcrumbs on both sides.

- Whisk the eggs and heat half a medium sized karahi with ghee or oil.

- Allow the ghee or oil to heat up. Dip 3 to 4 chops in the eggs and gently add them to the hot liquid in the karahi. Turn only once and remove from the heat when golden and red. Fry in 2 to 3 batches.

- Fry only just before serving.

- Serve with kando-papeto (onion and potato mixture recipe given in Jamva Chaloji No. 1) and brun pau.

PAPETA-NA-SUKKA-RAS-MA-CHAAP
(Potatoes and Chops in Dry Gravy)

10 double chops
4 potatoes, peeled and cut into
   8 pieces
2 onions, finely chopped
2 large tomatoes, finely chopped
2 pieces celery, 3" long each
½ cup chopped fresh coriander
½ tsp. turmeric powder
1 tsp. red chilli powder
1" piece cinnamon
3 bay leaves
2 mace flowers, finely ground
Salt
Ghee or oil

Preparation time	:	7 mins.
Cooking time	:	30-45 mins.
Serves	:	5

- Salt the chops.

- Place the onions and 3 tablespoons of oil in a pressure cooker over a medium heat. Cook till soft and brown. Add the cinnamon, bay leaves, cardamom seeds, cloves and the chops and stir up and down for 5 minutes.

- Then add the tomatoes, potatoes, celery, fresh coriander, turmeric and chilli powders and some salt. Stir for 5 more minutes, add sufficient water and cook till tender.

- If there is too much gravy, dry it off by transferring the potatoes and chops into a pan and placing it on a medium heat.

- Serve with peti pau and a green salad.

KESARWALA CHAAP
(Saffron Chops)

12 double chops
1 gm. saffron
1 ground onion
½ cup curds
8 red chillies, deseeded ⎤
7 black peppercorns   ⎫ Grind fine
1" piece cinnamon   ⎬ in little
½ tsp. mace powder   ⎭ water
½ tsp. cardamom seeds ⎦

Preparation time	:	15 mins.
Cooking time	:	30-40 mins.
Serves	:	6

- Heat the saffron on an iron tava till crisp. Crumble into the curds and mix well.

- Clean the chops with a damp cloth. Beat the fleshy portion with a meat mallet to soften the stringy, Indian mutton.

- Apply the ground masala to the chops. Then whisk the curds lightly and pour it over the chops and allow to marinade for 2 hours.

- Place ½ cup of ghee in a flat vessel over a medium heat. When the oil is hot, add the ground onion and fry till red brown. Then add the chops one by one and cover and cook over a slow fire. Remove the cover and cook till the chops are tender and bright red in colour. Remove from the fire and serve hot.

- Serve with potato chips and eat hot straight from the pan.

KHARA CHAAP
(Plain Chops)

10 double chops
1½ tsps. ginger-garlic paste
1 tsp. coarsely ground black
    peppercorns
1 large tomato, peeled and thickly
    sliced
Salt
Pure Ghee

Preparation time	:	5 mins.
Cooking time	:	45-55 mins.
Serves	:	5

- Wash and dry the chops. Then beat them with a meat tenderizer.

- Apply salt, pepper and ginger-garlic paste and keep aside for an hour.

- Take a heavy based frying pan or open-mouthed vessel. Put in 2 tablespoons of ghee. Place over medium heat and when hot, add the chops one by one and turn over to seal in the juice. Then lower the heat and add 1 cup of water and allow the chops to cook till tender.

- When all the water has dried up, check for tenderness. If necessary, add a little more water and cook some more. Our meat does not cook easily.

- When the meat is tender, spread the thick slices of tomato on top of the chops. Cook till soft and serve whilst still hot.

GOS-NU-ACHAAR
(Pickled Mutton)

1500 gms. boneless mutton
20 Kashmiri chillies,
   deseeded
4 large cloves of garlic   Grind
3 tbsps. cumin   fine in
15 black peppercorns   1 cup of
1" cinnamon   vinegar
3 cardamom seeds only
3 cloves
4 slit green chillies
2 bottles pure sugarcane vinegar
Coarse salt
Sesame Oil

Preparation time	: 15 mins.
Cooking time	: 1 hr. 15 mins. to
	1 hr. 30 mins.
Serves	: 20

- Wash the mutton well and salt it and set aside. After the masala is ready, apply it to the mutton pieces. Pour any left over vinegar onto the mutton and marinade for 4 hours.

- Take a large flat-bottomed vessel or karahi. Add 2 cups of oil to it and place over a medium flame. When hot, drop in the green chillies, wait for 2 minutes, and then add the masala and lower the flame and mix vigorously for 7 minutes. Add 1 bottle vinegar, keep over a very low fire and allow to simmer. When the vinegar has dried up, test for salt and tenderness. If the mutton is still tough, add half a bottle of vinegar and simmer. If it is not yet soft, add the last remaining half bottle and simmer till the mutton has become soft.

- Cool. Mix well and bottle.

DAHI-KESAR-NU-GOS

(Mutton Cooked in Saffron and Curds)

1 kg. mutton chunks with nali, washed
4 medium sized onions, finely chopped
1 tbsp. ginger-garlic paste
1 tbsp. garam masala
1 tsp. mace powder
1 tsp. broiled coriander seed powder
10 Kashmiri chillies, deseeded and ground in water
1 tsp. turmeric powder
300 gms. thick curds
½ cup sugar
1 gm. saffron
Salt
Pure ghee

Preparation time	:	10 mins.
Cooking time	:	35 mins.
Serves	:	6-8

- Add salt and ginger-garlic paste to the mutton.

- Place 3 tablespoons of ghee in a large flat-bottomed vessel and place on medium heat. Add the onions and cook till soft and pink.

- Add the ground chillies and all the masala powders and mix well for 3 minutes. Then add the mutton chunks, lower the flame, and cover and allow the mutton to cook in its own juice for 7 minutes. Open the vessel and stir vigorously and put in a pressure cooker with sufficient water and cook till the mutton is soft and tender.

- Once the mutton is cooked, put it in a clean vessel. If you feel the gravy is too much, then cook it over a low flame and allow it to dry up.

- Place the saffron strands on an iron tava and push it back and forth with a soft, crushed piece of old muslin. The fire must be low so that the saffron does not burn.

- Whisk the curds and the sugar together.

- When you have a thick gravy left in the vessel, gently add the whisked curds to the mutton and swing the vessel with 2 pieces of cloth, one in each hand. Swing the vessel in a rotating movement. Crush the heated strands of saffron between your fingers and sprinkle over the mutton. Stir as described above without a spoon. Simmer for 5 minutes and remove from the fire.

- Serve hot with parathas, fried potato halves and a lettuce and onion ring salad with a lemon dressing.

PAPETI-MA-GOS

(Mutton Cooked with Baby Potatoes)

750 gms. mutton leg chunks
250 gms. baby potatoes
200 gms. onions, finely chopped
200 gms. tomatoes, skinned and
    chopped
100 gms. carrot sticks, 1" long
2 stalks celery, cut into 2" pieces
4 green chillies, slit and deseeded
1 tbsp. ginger-garlic paste
1 tsp. turmeric powder
1½ tsp. chilli powder
1 tsp. maida
7 black peppercorns ⎫
2 green cardamom seeds ⎬ Dry grind
1 star anise ⎭ fine
Salt
Pure ghee

Preparation time	:	12 mins.
Cooking time	:	45-50 mins.
Serves	:	4-6

- Boil the potatoes in salted water with a pinch of turmeric. When half cooked, remove from the water, drain, and skin them.

- Wash the mutton twice, apply salt and the ginger-garlic paste and set aside.

- Place the onions in a vessel with 3 tablespoons of ghee and fry the onions till golden red. Add the maida and fry it for 2 minutes and then add the mutton and allow it to cook in its own juice for 7 minutes. Add the tomatoes, celery, green chillies, turmeric and chilli powders and the ground masala. Simmer for another 7 minutes. Then add 4 cups of water and place in the pressure cooker till the meat becomes soft and tender.

- Salt the boiled baby potatoes very lightly and deep fry in oil till golden in colour. Remove from heat.

- Remove the cooked meat in a clean pan, dry the gravy if necessary, and add the fried potatoes. Simmer for 5 minutes and serve hot.

- A green salad with fresh pineapple and soft bakery "ladi pau" will go well with this dish.

MOTTI-KAKRI-NI-BURYANI

(Large Marrow Gravy Cooked with Mutton and Eaten with Rice)

1 huge marrow, weighing 1 to
  1½ kg.
1500 gms. good leg mutton with
  nali, cut into chunks
500 gms. onions, cut into half and
  finely sliced
4 large tomatoes, skinned and
  chopped fine
6 slit green chillies, deseeded
1 tbsp. ground ginger-garlic paste
1½ tsps. ground black peppercorns
1½ tsps. turmeric powder
1 tsp. garam masala
1 cup finely chopped coriander
  leaves
15 chopped mint leaves
3 sprigs curry leaves
Salt
Pure ghee or Peanut oil

Preparation time	:	20 mins.
Cooking time	:	50-55 mins.
Serves	:	6-8

- Wash the mutton well and marinade in the ginger-garlic paste, black pepper powder and salt. Skin and chop the marrow into 1" pieces. Discard the soft portion containing the seeds.

- Take a large dekchi and put in ½ cup of pure ghee or oil and place over a medium heat. Add the finely sliced onions and cook till golden in colour. Then add the marinated mutton and cook in its own juice for 7 minutes. After that, add the slit green chillies and tomatoes, cook for 5 more minutes, and then add the marrow pieces and ½ litre of water and cook in a pressure cooker till soft and tender.

- When cooked, empty out into a large vessel and if you have too much gravy, burn it up a little. Taste for salt. Sprinkle the garam masala onto the cooked mutton and marrow along with the finely chopped coriander and mint. Simmer for 5 more minutes. The marrow should be totally mashed.

- Serve with white ghee rice or brown wagharela rice, pickles and papads.

BAWAJI-NU-BHUJAN

(Grandfather's Barbecued Mutton or Chicken)

1 kg. boneless mutton or chicken
2 cups whisked curds
2 tbsps. ginger-garlic paste
3 tsps. red chilli powder
Salt
Ghee

- Marinade the boneless mutton or chicken pieces overnight in the refrigerator after mixing them first with the ginger-garlic paste and then the chilli powder and whisked curds.

- The next day, light a fire with wood or coals and allow it to die down to white, hot embers. Add the salt now. Place the marinated pieces on thin skewers over 2 Y shaped sticks and cook till red hot and tender. Brush with a piece of cloth dipped in melted pure ghee.

Preparation time	:	20 mins.
Cooking time	:	45 mins. to 1 Hr.
Serves	:	10

- Do not allow the pieces to burn or blacken.

- Serve with hot drinks.

BAKRA-NI-MUNDI

(Goat's Head)

2 goat's heads. Get your butcher to clean them well for you and get him to chop them into decent sized pieces – at least 2" in size. Wash them thoroughly with flour, twice, and once again in plain water. Add salt and set aside
5 large onions, finely chopped
1½ tbsps. ginger-garlic paste
1 tbsp. turmeric
1½ tbsps. Kashmiri chilli paste
1½ tbsps. Parsi dhansakh masala
2 tsps. garam masala
4 green chillies, deseeded and chopped
½ cup chopped fresh coriander
Salt
Ghee

- Place the onions in a large vessel and cook in ½ cup ghee till golden brown.

- Apply the ginger-garlic paste to the cut goats' head pieces.

- Add the turmeric, chilli powder and the dhansakh masala, stir for 3 minutes and add the mutton head pieces. Stir for 5 minutes and add 2 litres of water and place on a low fire and allow to simmer for an hour till tender and the water has evaporated.

- Serve hot sprinkled with green chillies and coriander.

Preparation time	:	10 mins.
Cooking time	:	1 hour
Serves	:	4-6

BHAJI-MA-GOS

(Mutton Cooked in Spinach)

500 gms. boneless meat cut into tiny cubes not larger than ½"

2 bunches of chowlai bhaji, washed twice

1 bunch of palak bhaji, washed twice

½ bunch fresh coriander leaves, washed twice

1 tbsp. crushed ginger

4 large onions, finely chopped

2 large tomatoes, skinned and finely chopped

1 tbsp. crushed, deseeded green chillies

1 tbsp. coarsely crushed cumin seeds

1 tsp. turmeric powder

1 tsp. garam masala powder

Salt

Ghee

Preparation time	:	15 mins.
Cooking time	:	40-50 mins.
Serves	:	6-8

- Place 2 finely chopped onions in a pressure cooker along with 2 tablespoons of ghee. Allow the onions to turn pink and soft and then add the crushed ginger and stir for 2 minutes. Add the chopped mutton and salt and the required amount of water and cook till tender.

- Place 2 finely chopped onions in a pan along with 2 tablespoons of ghee and cook over a medium flame till soft and pink. Add the chillies, tomatoes, cumin and turmeric powder. Add a little salt.

- Cut the washed chowlai, palak and coriander leaves very fine and add them to the onions. Lower the heat and allow to cook till tender. Do not cover the vessel.

- Put the cooked mutton in a large vessel and mix in the cooked bhaji. Allow to simmer till all the mutton soup and bhaji water evaporates and a thick mixture is left in the vessel. Sprinkle the garam masala over the mutton and spinach, mix and serve hot.

- This dish is served with hot rotlis and an egg akuri.

BHARUCHI-BHAJI-DANA-NU-GOS

(Mutton with Green Peas and Spinach Bharuchi Style)

1 kg. mutton chunks
500 gms. fresh green peas, washed
6 bunches chowlai bhaji
1 bunch suva (dill) bhaji
1 bunch large leafed fenugreek bhaji
1 bunch fresh coriander leaves
350 gms. chopped onions
1½ tablespoons ginger-garlic paste
1 tbsp. black pepper powder
1 tbsp. garam masala powder
1½ tsps. turmeric powder
1½ tsps. red chilli powder
2-3 tsps. sugar
Juice of 3 sour limes
Salt
Ghee

Preparation time	:	20 mins.
Cooking time	:	40-50 mins.
Serves	:	6-8

- Wash all the bhajis twice, pluck the leaves only and chop fine.

- Marinade the mutton after washing it twice in salt and the ginger-garlic paste.

- Take 250 gms. of the chopped onions and cook them in ghee in a pressure cooker. When pink and soft, add the marinated mutton and the black pepper powder, sufficient water and cook till soft and tender.

- Place the remaining chopped onions in a vessel with 2 tablespoons of ghee. Cook the onions till soft and add the washed fresh green peas. Stir in the bhajis and lower the heat to simmer. Add the turmeric and chilli powders and stir and cook till soft. If the water released by the leaves is not enough to cook the peas, keep sprinkling a little at a time till they are soft.

- Place the cooked meat into the vessel containing the bhajis. Allow to simmer in order to let the soup evaporate and you have a thick rich dish in front of you. Taste for salt.

- Serve with curds and parathas.

KHARA-GOS-MA-KAMODIYO KAND

(Simple Meat Gravy cooked with Purple Yam)

Purple Yam is one of the most delicious root vegetables available to us. It is an expensive commodity and not usually available.

750 gms. leg mutton chunks with
   nali 1¼" square
500 gms. purple yam
2 large onions, finely chopped
2 tomatoes, skinned, deseeded
   and finely chopped
2 tsps. ginger-garlic paste
3 green cardamom
seeds only
10 black peppercorns
2 cloves   } Dry grind fine
½" piece cinnamon
1 tbsp. cumin seeds
1 tbsp. aniseeds
Salt
Ghee/Oil

- Skin the yam and cut it up into 1½" squares. Soak in salted water for 15 minutes and then parboil. Drain.

- Place the onions in a pressure cooker along with 3 tablespoons ghee and cook till golden red over a medium flame. Add the meat and fry in its own juice for 7 minutes and stir well. Add 3½ cups of water and cook the meat until tender.

- Heat a karahi half filled with oil and place on medium heat. When hot, fry the purple yam till it is tender.

- Place the cooked meat in a tapeli. If too much gravy is left, dry it off by putting it on simmer. When sufficient gravy is left, taste for salt. Add the fried yam, simmer for 5 minutes and remove from the fire.

- Serve hot with bread or rotis and a light egg dish and sweet chutney.

Preparation time	:	10 mins.
Cooking time	:	40-45 mins.
Serves	:	6-8

Malai Barfi (1)
Dried White Peas with
Cucumber and Raw Mangoes (2)
Wheat Flour Rotli (3)

TAMBOTA-NU-GOS

(Mutton Cooked in Tomatoes)

600 gms. ripe red tomatoes, skinned
500 gms. mutton chunks with nali
3 onions, finely chopped
1 tbsp. ginger-garlic paste
8 Kashmiri chillies, ground in water
2 pieces of 1" of cinnamon
3 bay leaves
3 green cardamoms, lightly crushed
3 cloves
7 peppercorns, lightly bruised
1 tsp. sugar
Salt
Peanut oil

Preparation time	:	18 mins.
Cooking time	:	40-45 mins.
Serves	:	6

- Wash and salt the mutton and apply the ginger-garlic paste.

- Place the onions in a pressure cooker with 3 tablespoons oil and place on a medium fire and cook till light brown.

- Add the whole masala, cinnamon, bay leaves, cardamoms, cloves and black peppercorns to the onions and mix well. Then add the ground chillies and stir briskly for 2 minutes and then add the mutton chunks. Fry non-stop for 5 minutes, then add 2½ cups of water and cover and cook till the mutton is tender.

- Remove the mutton along with its soup to a large patia. Cut each tomato into 4 large pieces and add to the mutton soup. Place on a very low fire and allow to simmer till the gravy becomes thick and red. Taste for salt. Sprinkle the sugar and mix gently and remove from the fire. If you feel it is necessary, add more sugar.

- Serve with soft peti pau along with french fries and fresh lettuce leaves.

Buttered Prawns in Green Chillies
and Mustard Seeds (1)
Soonamai's Eggs on Cream (2)

PAPAU-MA-GOS

((Mutton Cooked in Papaya Gravy)

1 large, firm ripe papaya
500 gms. mutton chunks
1½ tsps. ginger-garlic paste
2 large tomatoes, skinned, chopped
    fine
3 large Kashmiri chillies, with the
    twigs on
3 medium onions, cut fine
1 tsp. turmeric powder
3 tsps. garam masala
Salt
Ghee

Preparation time	:	8 mins.
Cooking time	:	45-50 mins.
Serves	:	6

- Wash the mutton chunks twice and marinade them in the ginger-garlic paste.

- Place the onions in the pressure cooker with 2 tablespoons of ghee and cook till brown. Add the whole red chillies, turmeric powder and the garam masala. Cook for 2 minutes and add the mutton. Lower the flame and stir the mutton for 5 to 7 minutes. Then add the finely chopped tomatoes and mix everything together for 5 minutes. Add sufficient water to cook the mutton and close the pressure cooker and allow to cook till the mutton is tender.

- Remove the cooked mutton into a patia or langri.

- Skin the papaya, remove the seeds and the inner furry pulp and cut it into 1" squares. Add them to the mutton and place the langri on a low fire. Allow to simmer for 12 to 15 minutes, stirring at least thrice.

- Serve hot with parathas and lime pickle.

MASOOR-NE-TARELA-LASAN-MA-GOS

(Black Lentils and fried Garlic with Mutton)

400 gms. kala masoor, soaked for
   ½ hour
700 gms. mutton chunks, washed
   twice
3 onions, chopped fine
6 tomatoes, chopped fine
2 tbsps. Parsi dhansakh masala
1 tbsp. Kairi sambhar
1 tbsp. red chilli powder
1½ tsps. turmeric powder
2 tbsps. jaggery, crushed ⎤
4 tbsps. sugarcane vinegar ⎦ Mix well
6 green chillies, deseeded,
   chopped fine
½ cup coriander, freshly chopped
½ cup sliced garlic
Salt
Ghee

Preparation time	:	12 mins.
Cooking time	:	45-50 mins.
Serves	:	8

- Place 3 tablespoons of ghee in a large tapeli. Add the onions and place on a low fire until they are cooked to a golden brown. Then toss in the meat and the washed kala masoor and cook for 3 minutes. Add the dhansakh masala, Kairi sambhar, chilli and turmeric powders. Mix well for 3 minutes. Add the tomatoes, mix and cover for 5 minutes.

- Add salt and place into a pressure cooker along with 5 cups of water. Cook until the mutton is soft and very tender. Empty out the cooker's contents into a large vessel and keep on simmering over a very low flame.

- Fry the garlic slices and green chillies in 1 tablespoon of ghee. Add the chopped coriander and pour all 3 items along with any remaining ghee over the simmering mutton and masoor. Simmer for 10 minutes.

- Add the mixed vinegar and jaggery and simmer for 5 minutes more.

- Serve with vegetable cutlets and bread.

GOS-NI-BOTI-MA-JEENA-KAVAB

(Masala Tiny Pieces of Mutton served with Baby Meatballs)

700 gms. leg mutton with nali separated and the meat cut boneless into ½" cubes
300 gms. minced mutton
350 gms. onions, cut fine
2 medium potatoes, boiled
½ cup finely chopped coriander leaves
6 green chillies, deseeded and finely chopped
2 tbsps. ginger-garlic paste
¾ tsp. turmeric powder
1 tsp. chilli powder
1 tsp. Parsi dhansakh masala
2 tsps. garam masala
2-3 eggs
100 gms. seedless raisins, cleaned and washed
150 gms. whole almonds, lightly fried
Salt
Ghee/Oil

- Wash the boneless mutton pieces along with the nali and marinade in salt and 1½ tablespoons ginger-garlic paste.

- Fry 300 gms. of onions in the pressure cooker in 3 tablespoons of ghee. When golden coloured, add the mutton pieces and allow to cook in its own juice for 5 minutes. Add the garam masala. Cook for 4 more minutes mixing the mutton and masala well. Add 3½ cups of water and cook till tender in the pressure cooker.

- Mash the potatoes in a thali till soft. No lumps should be there. Put in the minced mutton. Salt it and apply ½ a tablespoon of ginger-garlic paste. Mix well with the potato. Add 50 gms. of finely chopped onions, green chillies, coriander, turmeric and chilli powders. Mash and mix well and make into a large ball.

- Whisk 2 eggs. Make a depression into the minced meat and potato ball. Pour in the eggs and mix well. If the eggs are small or the mixture is too dry, whisk in the third egg, if required.

- Heat ½ a karahi of oil on high heat. When hot, lower the flame a little. Take the mince mixture in your left palm and with the fingers of your right hand, make tiny kababs as large as marbles and put them in the hot oil. Fry in batches so they cook well. When red, remove from the hot oil.

- Meanwhile, just before making the kababs, empty out the cooked mutton pieces with their gravy into a vessel and place on low heat to simmer. As soon as the kababs are fried, drain the oil and place directly into the mutton gravy along with the washed raisins. Simmer only for 5 minutes.

- Serve meat gravy with the kababs on a flat dish and top with whole fried almonds.

- Serve with rotlis or brun pau or French bread along with a green salad.

Preparation time	:	15 mins.
Cooking time	:	45-55 mins.
Serves	:	6-8

FARAJ-BEEJ-MA-KAVAB
(Meatballs in Sautéed Frenchbeans)

500 gms. frenchbeans, topped, tailed and sliced into julienne strips
300 gms. mutton mince
350 gms. onions, finely chopped
1 tbsp. ginger-garlic paste
1 tsp. finely chopped ginger
1 tsp. finely chopped garlic
1 tsp. turmeric powder
2 tsps. Parsi dhansakh masala
6 Kashmiri chillies ⎤ Grind fine
7 black peppercorns ⎥ with a
1 star anise ⎥ little
3 green cardamom seeds ⎦ water
2 eggs
8 slices bread
10 mint leaves
Breadcrumbs
Salt
Ghee/Oil

- Wash the cut frenchbeans and allow to drain in a colander.

- Take 300 gms. finely chopped onions and put them in a pressure cooker along with 3 tablespoons of ghee and cook to a light pink colour over medium heat. Add the ground ginger-garlic paste and fry for 3 minutes and then add the frenchbeans and salt along with the required water. Cook till tender and then empty the frenchbeans into a clean vessel.

- Take a thali and put in the mince. Add the chopped ginger and garlic, 50 gms. of finely chopped onions, turmeric and Parsi dhansakh masala powders and the ground masala. Mix well. Dip the bread slices into water and squeeze out the water and sprinkle the bread over the mince. Add salt and mix everything well with the mince. Whisk the eggs and add them to the mince mixture.

- Place the vegetable on a very low flame and allow to simmer.

- Place a karahi ½ filled with oil on high heat. When hot, lower the flame a little. Take the mince mixture in your left palm and with the fingers of your right hand, make tiny kababs as large as marbles and put them in the hot oil. Fry in batches so they cook well. When red, remove from the hot oil.

- Meanwhile, just before frying the kababs, place the vessel containing frenchbean gravy on low heat to simmer. As soon as the kababs are fried, drain the oil and place directly into the vegetable gravy. Simmer only for 5 minutes.

- Serve frenchbean gravy with the kababs on a flat dish, sprinkled with mint leaves.

- Serve with rotlis or brun pau or French bread along with a green salad.

Preparation time	:	18 mins.
Cooking time	:	40 mins.
Serves	:	6-8

TATRAVELI-PAPRI-MA-KAVAB

(Flat Beans with Meatballs)

500 gms. papri or flat beans
4 large onions
4 large tomatoes
1½ tsps. turmeric powder
2 tsps. chilli powder
2 tsps. Parsi Dhansakh Masala
1 tsp. ajwain or thymol seeds
2 whole pods garlic
1½" ginger
5 green chillies, deseeded ⎫
7 black peppercorns   ⎬ Grind fine
¾" cinnamon piece   ⎭
1 cup coriander leaves ⎦
½ cup crushed jaggery

For the Mince:

250 gms. mutton mince
1 tsp. ginger-garlic paste
1½ tsp. freshly ground black pepper
8 slices bread
2 eggs
Salt
Oil

Preparation time	:	18 mins.
Cooking time	:	35-40 mins.
Serves	:	4-6

- String the papri and cut each into 3 pieces. Wash, drain and set aside.

- Place the onions in a vessel with 3 tablespoons of oil on medium flame. Cook till pale pink and then add the ground masala and the tomatoes. Lower flame and cook for 5 minutes after which, add the papri, turmeric, chilli and Parsi dhansakh masala, the ajwain and 2 whole pods of garlic. Simmer for 5 minutes. Place in a steam cooker along with salt and a sufficient amount of water and cook till tender. Place in a clean vessel.

- Put the mince in a thali and mix in the ginger-garlic paste, black pepper powder and salt. Soak the bread slices in water and squeeze it out and mix the soaked, dried bread into the mince. Mix thoroughly.

- Whisk the eggs and mix them into the mince mixture and then form it into a ball.

- Heat a karahi half filled with oil. Heat over medium heat.

- Place the cooked papri on another stove on a very low heat to simmer.

- Wet your hands and make small balls out of the mince mixture and drop them directly into the hot oil in batches. Fry till golden brown and drop them directly into the simmering papri. When all the balls are fried, remove the papri from the fire and serve at once.

- Should be eaten with omelettes and rotlis.

KHATTO-MITTHO-KHEEMO-BHARELA TAMBOTA

(Sweet and Sour Mince Stuffed Tomatoes)

8 large firm red tomatoes,
  washed twice
400 gms. mutton
1 tbsp. ginger-garlic paste
1 tsp. turmeric powder
2 tsps. red chilli powder
2 tsps. garam masala
½ cup vinegar
½ cup sugar
3 tbsps. charoli
3 tbsps. seedless raisins
Salt
Ghee

Preparation time	:	15 mins.
Cooking time	:	40 mins.
Serves	:	6

- Cut the top of the tomatoes with a sharp knife and scoop out the inner seeds and flesh with a sharp tiny teaspoon. Use the pulp in another recipe.

- Mix the mince with salt and the ginger-garlic paste.

- Place 2 tablespoons of ghee in a tapeli over a low flame and when hot, add the mince and fry for 5 minutes. Then add the turmeric and chilli powder and cook for 2 more minutes before adding ½ cup of water at a time and cooking the mince till tender. When the mince is soft and dry, add the vinegar, sugar, charoli and raisins and mix vigorously and simmer for 3 minutes more and remove from the fire.

- Slightly salt the tomatoes from the inside and fill up with the mince mixture.

- Heavily grease a round or rectangular pyrex dish. Place all the tomatoes neatly in it and place in the oven at 350ºF for 20 to 25 minutes, till the tomato shells have cooked. Add a sprinkling of water.

- Serve with black masoor or chana dal and bread.

OF MINCE STUFFED LARGE CUCUMBERS

Navsari is a very well-known town in Gujarat. Almost every Parsi knows that this is the place from where their vinegar and pickles come to Bombay. The whole industry is in the hands of 2 companies, K. F. Kolah and E. F. Kolah. They manufacture all sorts of mango and lemon pickles, chutneys and a very special fish roe pickle in mustard gravy.

Once you use their white and brown vinegars, you will never touch the synthetic stuff.

Soonamai, my great grandmother had no vegetables in her back yard in May. She had to wait for the monsoon to sow her seeds, after which, she was amply rewarded by a huge array of fresh coriander, ladyfingers, cucumbers and pumpkins. She dehydrated most of these vegetables. She chopped them up and dried them on the roof of her cottage and then sealed them up so that they could be used in the hot season and the monsoons.

I have noticed that, whenever housewives grew their own vegetables in their backyards, they used each vegetable in a variety of ways which baffles us today. They used the flowers, fruits, leaves, vines and even roots of certain vegetables. For instance, take the pumpkin vine. The flowers were deep fried and eaten, the fruit was cooked in a dozen ways, the tender vines were also skinned, cooked and consumed.

Colocassia leaves were used, cooked in various dals, made into vadis or large patrels, their stalks were skinned, cooked and eaten and the roots – well-known as arbi – were eaten, boiled, fried, cooked in curries and used as the base for cutlets.

Cucumbers galore grew in Soonamai's backyard, small ones and large ones, white ones and green ones. The largest size was skinned, the seeds removed and cooked and eaten as an accompaniment with rice and a piece of fried dried fish and mango pickle in oil. Sometimes, on very rare occasions, mostly Friday which was market day, the uncles Pirojsha and Nariman went to Maroli and bought goats' meat for the family. Maiji, as everyone lovingly called her, would separate the good chunks to be roasted and cooked for dinner with potatoes. The neck and shoulder portion was minced on a large block of wood which was the portion of a tree trunk, and used to make kheema, kababs and cutlets.

Now, to go back to the cucumbers. Very large, yet tender ones were selected and skinned. One end was sliced off cleanly and the cap set aside. With the help of a long, sharp knife, thinned over the years by use, the cucumber was hollowed out. Then salt and black pepper were mixed and then applied on the inside and outside of the cucumber and kept for 30 minutes in a cool place to allow the water to seep out. Then chilli-hot kheema was cooked, cooled and stuffed into the cucumbers, which were once again re-capped with the help of fine thin khajuri leaf sticks and cooked in ghee till well done. I am giving 2 methods of the type of kheema (mince) which was used for the stuffing.

3 large, 10" cucumbers, skinned and
    hollowed out
750 gms. of fresh mince, marinaded
    in salt and ginger-garlic
4 large onions
4 green chillies, deseeded ⎤
5 red chillies, deseeded   ⎟ Grind in
10 cloves, large garlic   ⎬ sugarcane
1 tbsp. cumin seeds   ⎟ vinegar
1 tbsp. Parsi dhansakh   ⎦
    masala
1 tsp. turmeric powder
2 sticks of curry leaves
Salt
Til oil

Preparation time	: To prepare the 3 cucumbers, 30 minutes
Cooking time	: 55 minutes
Serves	: Each 10" cucumber serves 3 persons

- Chop the onions and put them in a pan along with ½ cup of oil on a medium flame. Cook till soft and pink and then add the masala ground in vinegar. Stir well for 3 minutes and then add the mince and allow to simmer for 35 minutes till cooked. Keep sprinkling water on the mince and cook it to tenderness – but allow to dry.

- Taste the mince for salt and stuff it into the cucumbers. Recap with the chopped off slices and stick fine slivers of wood such as toothpicks to secure the caps to the cucumber.

- Take a flat vessel, thali or kuthrot. The latter is a kalai thali with high sides. Place 1 cup of til oil in its centre. Place on a medium flame and add the curry leaves. When they crackle, place the 3 cucumbers side by side in the centre of the kuthrot. You may need more oil. Take the cucumbers carefully between two flat, holed chamach and turn them upside down. Cover and cook over a low flame till tender and soft.

CUCUMBERS STUFFED
WITH MINCE, RAISIN AND NUTS

750 gms. mince, marinated in salt
   and ginger-garlic paste
200 gms. skinned, and chopped
   tomatoes
4 large onions, finely chopped
3 green chillies, deseeded and
   finely chopped
1 tsp. turmeric powder
1 tsp. garam masala
1 tsp. chilli powder
½ cup crushed jaggery
½ cup vinegar
½ cup finely chopped coriander
½ cup raisins, washed
¼ cup charoli nuts
Salt, Oil

Preparation time	:	30 mins.
Cooking time	:	55 mins.
Serves	:	9

- Prepare the cucumbers as described in the first recipe.

- Fry the onions in 3 tablespoons of oil till soft and pink in a large vessel. Add the marinated mince and mix well till it is dry and red.

- Add all the masalas and the tomatoes, coriander, raisins and nuts and mix well. Add 1 cup of water and allow to simmer till dry. Check for tenderness and salt. Add the vinegar and crushed jaggery and cook till dry.

- Stuff the cucumbers with the mince as described in recipe no.1. Recap the cucumbers and cook in hot oil in a kuthrot.

- Serve with vegetable pulao and green salad.

CUCUMBERS STUFFED WITH TOMATO MINCE

3 large cucumbers
4 onions, finely chopped
750 gms. minced mutton, marinated
   in salt and ginger-garlic paste
400 gms. skinned, finely chopped
   tomatoes
1 tsp. turmeric powder
1½ tsps. chilli powder
2 tsps. garam masala
½ cup fresh coriander,
   finely chopped
1 tsp. sugar
Salt, Oil

Preparation time	:	10 mins.
Cooking time	:	42 mins.
Serves	:	9

- Place 3 tablespoons of oil in a karahi and cook the onions in it till pink and soft. Put in the marinated mince and fry it till red and dry. Add all the masala powders and cook for 5 minutes. Then put in the tomatoes and mix well with the mince.

- Cook the mince over a low fire till tender. If necessary, add ½ cup of water along with the sugar and coriander. Let it simmer and become dry. Taste for salt.

- Stuff the skinned cucumbers as written in the previous recipe and cook till soft in a large kuthrot.

KHEEMO-BHARELU-PARVAL-TAMOTA-NI-GRAVY-MA

(Stuffed Snake Gourd in Tomato Gravy)

For the Snake Gourd:

3 large snake gourds, scrubbed off
    the white flaky skin and obtain
    10 pieces of the vegetable, each
    3" long
½ kg. sweet and sour cooked
    minced meat
3 mashed potatoes, salted
4 egg whisked with 1 tbsp. of
    cornflour
Breadcrumbs
Salt
Oil

For the Tomato Gravy:

10 large tomatoes, skinned,
    deseeded and pulped
1 large onion, finely chopped
1 tsp. red chilli powder
1 tsp. coarsely ground cumin seeds
1 tbsp. sugar
Salt
Oil

Preparation time	:	20 mins.
Cooking time	:	40-60 mins.
Serves	:	4-6

- Clean the snake gourd pieces of the fluff within them and wash and dry them.

- Stuff the pieces with the dried mince and plug them on both sides with mashed potatoes.

- Place a karahi ½ filled with oil on medium heat.

- Meanwhile whisk the eggs with 1 tablespoon of cornflour.

- When the oil heats up, roll the snake gourd pieces in breadcrumbs and then dip a few at a time in the whisked eggs and deep fry till golden brown. When all the pieces have been fried, set them up in a warm place.

- Put 1 tablespoon of the vegetable fried oil in a tapeli. Add the onions and allow to turn pink. Add the chilli powder and crushed cumin, stir for 2 minutes and add the tomato pulp, sugar and salt to taste. Cook for 7 minutes over a very low fire.

- Empty the tomato sauce onto a flat dish and neatly arrange the fried rolls on top of it.

- Serve with bread slices and a sweet and sour mango chutney.

GOS-NI-CHANA-SING-NI-CURRY

(Mutton Curry with Grams and Peanuts)

750 gms. of mutton chunks, washed
1 freshly grated coconut ⎤
12 Kashmiri chillies,
  deseeded
2 medium sized onions,
  grated   Grind
½ cup skinned grams   very
½ cup skinned peanuts   fine in
½ cup broiled coriander   water
  seeds
2 tbsps. sesame seeds
2 tbsps. poppy seeds ⎦
½ cup tamarind juice
15 curry leaves
Salt
Refined oil

Preparation time	:	20 mins.
Cooking time	:	35-40 mins.
Serves	:	6-8

- Salt the mutton chunks.

- Cook the washed, salted mutton in a pressure cooker till soft and tender. Reserve the soup and mutton separately.

- Grind the masala till soft and buttery.

- Place 2 tablespoons of oil and the curry leaves in a vessel, over medium heat. Allow the leaves to crackle and then add the masala and stir vigorously for 7 minutes till red and hot. Then add the cooked mutton, lower the flame, and allow to simmer for 3 minutes. Add the strained mutton soup and extra water to make up the amount of curry you want. Simmer for 10 minutes and remove from fire.

- Serve with white rice, papads and an onion and cucumber kachumber.

KAJU-GOS-NI-CURRY
(Mutton and Cashew Nut Curry)

500 gms. mutton chunks with nali, washed twice

1 fresh large coconut, grated ⎤

10-12 Kashmiri chillies, deseeded

2 tbsps. broiled dhania

1 tbsp. broiled poppy seeds ⎬ Grind very fine with ½ cup water

1 tbsp. broiled sesame seeds

1 tsp. broiled cumin seeds

1 lump tamarind, twice the size of a sour lime

¾ cup broken cashew nuts ⎦

4 slit green chillies, whole, deseeded

5 potatoes peeled and cut into 4 pieces each, washed

2 sprigs curry leaves

Salt

Peanut or Sunflower oil

Preparation time	:	20 mins.
Cooking time	:	25 mins.
Serves	:	6-8

- Salt the washed mutton and place it with the potatoes in a pressure cooker with sufficient water to make soup for the curry.

- Place 2 tablespoons oil and the curry leaves in a broad vessel. Put on medium heat. When the leaves crackle, add the finely ground masala, lower the flame and cook the masala till red. Add the slit green chillies.

- Add the mutton and potato pieces to the red curry masala and strain the soup into it through a sieve.

- Simmer for 10 to 12 minutes and serve with green peas rice and papads.

GOS-NU-ISTOO-MARCHAN-VAGAR

(Mutton Stew without Chillies)

750 gms. mutton chunks with nali
350 gms. fresh tomato puree
300 gms. baby potatoes, boiled and
  skinned
300 gms. baby onions, skinned
250 gms. frenchbeans, cut
  diagonally into thin slices
250 gms. baby carrots, cut into
  slices
250 gms. fresh green peas
2 green chillies (Optional)
2 tbsps. finely chopped parsley or
  celery stalks
2 tbsps. finely chopped fresh
  coriander
1 tbsp. ginger-garlic paste
2 tsps. freshly ground black
  peppercorns
2 tsps. coarsely ground coriander
  seeds
2 tsps. coarsely ground fennel seeds
1 tsp. crushed caraway seeds
2 tbsps. cornflour
1 tsp. sugar
Salt
Pure Ghee

Preparation time	:	25 mins.
Cooking time	:	45 mins.
Serves	:	6

- Wash the mutton and marinade in salt and the ginger-garlic paste.

- Place the pressure cooker on medium heat. Add 3 tablespoons of ghee and allow it to become hot. Then add the mutton and stir for 5 minutes. Allow it to sizzle well. Add 3 cups of water and cook till tender. Cool the cooker and place the mutton gravy in a large vessel.

- Boil the green peas and the frenchbeans separately in salted water with a pinch of soda-bi-carb. Drain the water when cooked and set aside.

- Boil the carrots in hot water and when tender, drain from the water and set aside.

- Deep fry the potatoes and onions, salt slightly and set aside.

- Take a deep vessel. Add 2 tablespoons of ghee and place over a stove on a medium flame. When hot, lower the flame and add the black pepper powder, the coriander and fennel seeds and stir in the ghee for 2 minutes. Add the tomato puree and allow to cook. Stir the cornflour in ½ cup of water and stir non-stop till it becomes thick and smooth. Add salt.

- Place the mutton gravy on a low fire and add all the boiled and fried vegetables to it. Then add the tomato puree with 1 teaspoon of sugar. Allow to simmer for 10 minutes.

- Serve hot sprinkled with the coriander leaves.

- If liked, deseed and finely chop 2 green chillies and sprinkle over the stew.

EGGS

SEKTA-NA-MAVA-PER-EEDA

(Eggs on Drumstick Pulp)

6 eggs
2 cups boiled, drumstick pulp
2 onions, sliced and deep fried
1 large tomato, skinned and
    chopped fine
1 tsp. green chillies, chopped fine
2 tbsps. fresh coriander, chopped
    fine
½ tsp. turmeric powder
½ tsp. black pepper powder
Salt
Pure ghee

Preparation time	:	20-25 mins.
Cooking time	:	35 mins.
Serves	:	6

- Place 2 tablespoons of pure ghee in a large iron frying pan, non-stick pan or a small thali. Place the ghee on a low fire and add the tomato, green chillies, coriander, turmeric and black pepper powders and cook till the tomato is pulpy and soft and not watery. Add the drumstick pulp and salt and simmer for 4 more minutes, stirring all the while.

- Reduce the flame and make 6 depressions in the drumstick pulp and crack an egg in each hollow. Sprinkle with fine salt and a little water and cover and cook till firm.

- Serve with rice flour rotlis.

KOTHMIR-KANDA-PER-EEDA

(Eggs on Onions and Fresh Coriander)

5 eggs, whisked
6 onions, cut into half and finely
    sliced and deep fried
2 bunches coriander leaves,
    plucked, washed and finely
    chopped
6 green chillies, deseeded and
    finely chopped
1 bunch fresh garlic cleaned,
    washed and finely chopped
1 tsp. turmeric powder
1 tsp. black pepper powder
Salt
Peanut oil

Preparation time	:	20 mins.
Cooking time	:	20 mins.
Serves	:	4-6

- Take a large frying pan or thali like vessel. Add 2 tablespoons of oil and cook the fresh garlic and chillies in it. Once the garlic has softened, add the turmeric and the black pepper powder and stir for 2 minutes. Add the deep fried onions, stir for 5 minutes over a low heat and spread it out at the bottom of the frying pan or thali. Sprinkle fine salt.

- Whisk the eggs well.

- Place the frying pan on simmer and pour over the whisked eggs. Cover and cook till set.

- Serve cut into wedges along with hot spicy bean or dal dish.

TOORIA-PER-EEDA

(Eggs on Ridge Gourd)

8 eggs
1 kg. ridge gourd
250 gms. onions
6 green chillies, deseeded and
  chopped fine
4 large tomatoes, skinned and
  chopped fine
1 tsp. turmeric power
1 tsp. chilli powder
½ tsp. black pepper powder
½ cup finely chopped coriander
  leaves
Salt
Ghee

Preparation time	:	15 mins.
Cooking time	:	20-22 mins.
Serves	:	4-6

- Taste each ridge gourd for bitterness. Then skin them very lightly and cut them into 4 long pieces and then chop them wafer thin.

- Cut the onions into halves and slice them finely. Place them in a large flat thali type vessel with 3 tablespoons of ghee and cook till golden coloured. Add the ridge gourd, green chillies, tomatoes, turmeric, chilli and black pepper powders. Allow to simmer till the mixture has softened and is pulpy. Add salt. Mix in the coriander and remove from the fire.

- Just before you eat, place the pan on simmer. When the vegetable becomes hot, make 8 depressions in the vegetable layer and crack an egg in each one. Cover and cook till the eggs become firm; or whisk the eggs over the vegetable, cover and cook till firm.

- Serve with ladi bread or rotlis for breakfast or lunch or dinner.

MAWA-NE-TAMBOTA-PER-EEDA

(Eggs on Mawa and Tomatoes)

12 eggs
150 gms. mawa
750 gms. tomatoes, skinned and
   finely chopped
300 gms. onions, finely chopped
½ bunch fresh coriander, washed,
   finely chopped
6 green chillies, deseeded, finely
   chopped
1 tsp. turmeric powder
2 tsps. red chilli powder
2 tsps. garam masala
2 tsps. sugar
Salt
Ghee

Preparation time	:	15 mins.
Cooking time	:	25 mins.
Serves	:	8-10

- Place 2 tablespoons of ghee in a large frying pan, add the onions and cook till brown on a medium flame. Add the tomatoes, coriander, green chillies, turmeric and red chilli powders, the garam masala, and stir vigorously for 2 minutes. Add the tomatoes and cook till they are soft and pulpy. Add salt to taste and crumble in the mawa with your finger tips. Cook over a low fire for 5 minutes till the mawa has mixed well with the tomatoes and then spread the mixture in a large thali or divide it between 2 large frying pans.

- Make 12 depressions in the tomato mixture and crack each egg carefully into its place. Sprinkle fine salt and add a little water on top of the eggs.

- Cover the vessel and place on a low flame till the eggs set.

- Serve as a breakfast dish with hot rice rotlis or wheat rotlis.

TAMBOTA-MA-BHARELI-AKOORI
(Tomatoes Stuffed with Akoori)

6 large, red, firm tomatoes
6 eggs
2 onions, very finely chopped
4 green chillies, deseeded and very
    finely chopped
2 tomatoes, skinned and very finely
    chopped
½ teacup coriander leaves, very
    finely chopped
½ tsp. turmeric powder
½ tsp. ground ginger-garlic paste
½ tsp. red chilli powder
10 gms. boiled, skinned, sliced
    almonds
10 gms. boiled, skinned, sliced
    pistachios
10 gms. washed, seedless raisins
Salt
Pure ghee

Preparation time	:	10 mins.
Cooking time	:	12-15 mins.
Serves	:	6

- Slice the tops of the tomatoes and with a sharp, tiny teaspoon, scoop out the pulp and seeds and keep aside for use.

- Take a karahi and place the onions in it. Add 2 tablespoons of pure ghee and place over a low flame till pink and soft. Add the ginger-garlic paste, stir for 2 minutes and then add the green chillies, tomatoes, turmeric and chilli powders and stir gently until the tomato has been reduced to a pulp. Add salt and thicken the mixture.

- Take a small karahi, put in 3 teaspoons of ghee and separately fry the almonds, pistachios and raisins and add them to the tomato mixture.

- Whisk the eggs with a pinch of salt and pour them into the cooked tomatoes and begin stirring over a low fire non-stop, until they are cooked. The eggs should be firm and not soft.

- Stuff this egg akoori into the tomato cups and then place them onto a greased pyrex dish and bake them at 350ºF for 15 to 20 minutes or until the tomatoes are soft. Add ¼ cup of water so the tomatoes cook thoroughly.

SOONAMAI-NA-MALAI-PER-EEDA
(Soonamai's Eggs on Cream)

Eggs were laid by the dozen in Soonamai's wada (compound). Cream was easy to lay hands on. When she had guests for lunch, all of a sudden, she normally served eggs as a side dish. The ones I liked best were her baked cream eggs. The malai was laid out in a flat bottomed terracotta dish with high sloping slides and it was placed on hot red wood over hot ashes. Then, in a small aluminium vessel, she heated butter and added green chillies to it. When the cream became hot, she broke as many as a dozen eggs into it and sprinkled them with salt. Then she took a tablespoon and drizzled the green chillies cooked in butter over the eggs and covered the vessel and allowed the eggs to simmer gently till firm.

Today, I make the same sort of eggs in a non-stick frying pan. The taste, is of course, not the same!!

8 eggs
300 gms. heavy cream
4 green chillies, deseeded and
   finely chopped
100 gms. butter
Salt

- Place the cream in a large non-stick frying pan over a low, gentle heat.

- In a small saucepan, heat the butter and add the green chillies and cook for 2 minutes. Remove from fire.

- When the cream gets hot, crack each egg separately into a saucer and slide it into the cream and sprinkle with fine salt.

- Cover the eggs for 2 minutes, then drizzle them with the butter and green chillies. Cover and cook till firm.

- Serve them with hot buttered toast or hot parathas.

Preparation time	:	7 mins.
Cooking time	:	15 mins.
Serves	:	6

MAIJI-NA-BAFELA-EEDA-NA-CUTLES

(Maiji's Boiled Egg Cutlets)

In Maiji's days, she used fine rawa or soji for frying her cutlets, kavabs, chops and vegetables. But, breadcrumbs are better for us today. They give a neat and golden appearance. If she got into the mood, she would come up with some delicious dishes with tantalizing aromas. She was very famous for making delicious, fairly light cutlets by using boiled eggs. The children would refuse to eat anything less than 4 or 5 pieces.

1 litre thick creamy milk
10 boiled eggs, shelled
2 raw eggs
4-5 tbsps. finely ground maida
    (Soonamai's maida was made out
    of her own home-grown wheat)
1 finely chopped onion
8 green chillies, deseeded and finely
    chopped
6 curry leaves, chopped
1 tsp. broiled crushed cumin seeds
1 tsp. black pepper powder
1 pinch red chilli powder
Salt
Ghee

Preparation time	:	15-20 mins.
Cooking time	:	30-35 mins.
Serves	:	6-8

- Heat the onion in a flat-bottomed vessel along with ½ cup of ghee till pink and soft. Add the curry leaves, green chillies, cumin and black pepper powders. Cook for 2 minutes and then add the maida. Lower the flame and mix vigorously and when the flour becomes ivory coloured, gradually add the milk in a thin stream, stirring all the while till you get a smooth thick sauce. It should be very tight. Just in case your sauce is liquidy, add more maida and cook all over again until you get a thick sauce.

- Add salt to the sauce and mix well. Whisk the 2 raw eggs and add to the mixture.

- Divide the boiled eggs into halves. Place the flat side on a cutting board and cut each half into 4 strips. Turn all the boiled egg strips into the white milk sauce. Taste for salt and spices. Cool in a refrigerator to harden the sauce.

- Place ghee in a karahi on a medium flame.

- Spread the breadcrumbs on a plastic or wooden board. Take a tablespoon of the boiled egg mixture and drop it upon the breadcrumbs. Cover completely with the breadcrumbs and shape into an oval shape with both your palms.

- When the ghee gets hot, drop 4 to 5 of these cutlets into it and fry gently till golden red.

GĀMTI AMLETTE
(Country Omelette)

10 eggs
2 mashed potatoes
1 small raw mango, peeled and
   finely chopped
1 medium sized onion, finely
   chopped
4-6 green chillies, deseeded and
   finely chopped
1 tbsp. grated fresh ginger
½ cup finely chopped coriander
½ tsp. turmeric
1 tsp. red chilli powder
1 tsp. sambhar masala
Salt
Ghee

Preparation time	:	12-15 mins.
Cooking time	:	25-30 mins.
Serves	:	8-10

- Take a rounded basin and crack the eggs into it. Whisk them well.

- Add the finely chopped mango, onion, grated ginger, chopped coriander, the masalas and salt and mix well.

- Mash the potatoes very fine and then add them to the whisked egg mixture.

- Heat 1 tablespoon ghee in an iron tava or a kalai karahi. When hot, pour in ½ cup of the mixture at a time. When brown at the bottom, turn over and cook the top side. You should have at least 10 to 14 omelettes out of this mixture.

- Each time you make a fresh omelette, mix the eggs well so that the mashed potato does not remain at the bottom of the basin.

- Serve hot with rotlis or brun pau.

Vegetables

NAVAJBAI FITTER-NA-KOPRA-NA-KAVAB

(Navajbai Fitter's Coconut Kababs)

2 coconuts, grated
3 onions, finely chopped
½ bunch fresh coriander leaves,
    washed and finely chopped
9 green chillies, deseeded and
    finely chopped
15 cloves garlic
1" piece ginger
1 tsp. turmeric powder
½ tsp. black pepper powder
½ tsp. Parsi dhansakh masala
5 desert spoons chana or gram
    aata
Salt, Ghee

Preparation time	:	20-25 mins.
Cooking time	:	25-30 mins.
Serves	:	8

- Except the gram flour and ghee, grind all the items on a grinding stone or a mixie. The masala must be very fine.

- Remove the masala into a bowl and mix in the chana aata. Taste for salt.

- Make one ball, slightly larger or the same size as a sour lime.

- Heat the ghee in a karahi over medium heat. When it heats up, add the masala ball and fry till golden brown. If by any chance it disintegrates, add some more aata.

- Fry all the balls gently in batches.

- Serve with masoor, sour lime and rotlis.

VAGHARELA-TINDORA

(Sautéed Gherkins)

450 gms. gherkins, topped and
    tailed and cut into fine slices
4 large onions, chopped
4 large tomatoes, skinned and
    chopped
½ grated fresh coconut
7 green chillies, deseeded ⎤
10 large cloves of garlic   Grind
1 tbsp. cumin seeds   fine with
5 black peppercorns   a little
½" piece cinnamon   water
1½ tsp. turmeric powder ⎦
Salt, Sesame oil

Preparation time	:	20 mins.
Cooking time	:	45-55 mins.
Serves	:	6

- Wash the gherkins and slice them fine. Place the onions in a tapeli and add 3 tablespoons of oil and place over a medium flame till soft and pink. Add the turmeric and ground masala and stir well for 3 minutes. Then add the sliced vegetable and coconut and salt. Cover and cook in its juice over a low fire.

- Add 2 cups of water, cover and allow to simmer till tender. If the water dries up, keep putting water on the lid and when it gets hot, pour into the vegetables. This is a very tasty vegetable, but it must be soft to eat.

- Serve with fried fish and amla chutney.

BEETROOT-NA-PATTICE
(Beetroot Patties)

500 gms. mashed potatoes, salted
6 beetroots, boiled in a pressure
   cooker with the skins on
1 deep fried onion
6 green chillies, deseeded and
   chopped fine
½ cup fresh coriander, chopped fine
½ cup cornflour, stirred in water
1 tsp. black pepper powder
½ cup sugarcane vinegar
½ cup sugar
4 eggs
Breadcrumbs
Salt
Refined sunflower oil

Preparation time	:	30 mins.
Cooking time	:	20-25 mins.
Serves	:	8-10

- Peel the beetroots and cut them into fine squares. Put them in a large pan.

- Place the pan over a low flame and add the fried onions, chillies, coriander, black pepper, vinegar and sugar and mix well. When the mixture is hot, sprinkle it with fine salt.

- Mix the cornflour with ½ cup of water and add it to the hot beetroot stirring all the time till it becomes sticky and thick and sufficiently tight. Taste for salt and remove from the fire and cool.

- Place the salted, mashed potatoes in a thali and knead them well. Then make 8 to 10 balls out of the potatoes.

- Grease your palms with oil and shape each potato ball into a flat saucer shape and stuff it with 1 tablespoon of the sweet and sour beetroot mixture and form into a pattice.

- Cover the pattice with breadcrumbs.

- Whisk the eggs in a soup plate.

- Heat ½ karahi of oil till hot. Dip the crumbed pattice into the whisked eggs and deep fry till golden brown.

- Serve hot at tea time or mealtimes.

FARAJBEEJ-NA-PATTICE
(Frenchbeans Patties)

500 gms. mashed potatoes
350 gms. frenchbeans, stringed
   and cut very fine
100 gms. grated fresh coconut
1 tsp. ginger-garlic paste
1 tsp. red chilli powder
1 tsp. dhansakh masala
½ tsp. turmeric powder
2 tbsps. tamarind pulp   ] Melt
2 tbsps. crushed jaggery   ] together
4 eggs
Breadcrumbs
Salt
Peanut oil

Preparation time	:	15 mins.
Cooking time	:	35-40 mins.
Serves	:	4-6

- Place 1 tablespoon of oil in a karahi and when hot, add the grated coconut, ginger-garlic paste, chilli, turmeric and dhansakh powders and cook for 2 minutes.

- Add the washed frenchbeans and lower the heat and add salt. Lower the heat, cook for 3 minutes, then add 1 cup of water, cover and cook till dry and soft. Add more water only if necessary. The vegetable must be dry.

- Add the tamarind-jaggery pulp and heat a little more till no water remains in the vegetables.

- Place the mashed potatoes in a thali. Salt them. Then make equal sized balls. Oil your palms, then place one ball of potato onto your left palm and press it into the shape of a saucer. Place 1 tablespoon of the frenchbeans in the center and close up the rest of the potato to make a firm covering.

- Heat ½ a karahi of oil.

- Place the breadcrumbs on a wooden board.

- Whisk the eggs in a soup plate.

- As soon as the oil heats up, cover the potato balls with breadcrumbs, dip into the egg and then gently put it into the hot oil. Fry 3 to 4 at a time till golden brown. Remove from the oil.

- Serve hot with chana dal and rotlis.

SAFED-SOOKKA-VATANA-KAKRI-NE-KACCHI-KERI

(Dried White Peas with Cucumber and Raw Mangoes)

300 gms. dried white peas, soaked
   overnight
2 onions, finely chopped
1 tbsp. ginger-garlic paste
1½ tsps. turmeric powder
1½ tsps. red chilli powder
5 green chillies, deseeded and
   chopped fine
1 piece 1" cinnamon
2 cloves
1 large thick cucumber, 6" long,
   skinned
3 green tender mangoes, skinned
   and each cut into 4 long pieces
2 sprigs curry leaves
Salt
Ghee

Preparation time	:	20 mins.
Cooking time	:	40-45 mins.
Serves	:	6-8

- Wash the dried peas twice and cook them in water, turmeric, ginger-garlic paste and salt, in a pressure cooker. They should be tender but whole.

- Place the onions and curry leaves in a broad vessel along with 2 tablespoons ghee over a low heat. When the onions become soft and brown, add the chilli and sambhar powders, the green chillies, cinnamon and cloves and cook for 3 minutes. Then add the cooked peas along with any leftover water and allow to boil. Taste for salt.

- Cut the white portion of the cucumber into 1½" sticks, ½" wide and add to the boiling peas. Add the mango pieces and lower the heat and allow to simmer till the mangoes are soft.

- Serve with rice rotlis and fried fish or mutton cutlets.

PAKKI-KERI-NI-TARKARI
(Cooked Ripe Mangoes)

7 ripe mangoes, peeled, chopped
½ tsp. mustard seeds
½ tsp. coriander seeds, broiled and
   coarsely ground
6 green chillies, deseeded and slit
2 tbsps. crushed jaggery (optional)
6 curry leaves
Salt
Pure ghee

Preparation time	:	7 mins.
Cooking time	:	9 mins.
Serves	:	4-6

- Place 2 tablespoons of pure ghee in a heavy-bottomed pan over medium heat. After 3 minutes, add the curry leaves, mustard seeds, coriander seeds and slit green chillies and allow to crackle.

- Mix lightly, lower the flame, and add the crushed jaggery. When it melts, sprinkle the ripe mango pieces over it and add a little salt. Mix well, cover and allow to simmer for 5 minutes.

- Serve hot, straight from the pan, as an accompaniment to vegetables, dals or a fish dish.

- Best eaten with hot, rice flour rotlis.

BHAJI-MA-SOOKKA-DANA
(Dried Green Peas Cooked in Spinach)

250 gms. dried green peas, soaked
   overnight
3 bunches chowlai bhaji, washed
   twice
2 bunches palak bhaji, washed twice
1 bunch suva (dill) bhaji, washed
   twice
1½ tsps. turmeric powder
350 gms. chopped onions
1½" ginger ⎤
10 large cloves garlic ⎥
1 tbsp. cumin seeds ⎥ Grind
4-6 green chillies, deseeded ⎥ fine
15 black peppercorns ⎦
Salt
Ghee

Preparation time	:	30 mins.
Cooking time	:	30 mins.
Serves	:	6-8

- Cook the dried beans, after washing them well, in salt and a pinch of turmeric till tender. The peas should be intact, not mushy.

- Place the onions in a large vessel along with 3 tablespoons of ghee and cook till soft and pink over a medium flame. Add the turmeric and put in the ground masala and keep stirring for 3 minutes. Chop the 3 different bhajis fine and add them to the masala. Drain the beans from the water and add them along with the spinach.

- Allow to simmer over a slow fire till the bhaji is cooked and dry.

- Serve with fried fish, chopped pineapple salad and rotlis.

PAKELI-KERI-NO-PULAO

(Ripe Mango Pulao)

For the Rice:

450 gms. basmati rice
2 fried onions
1 gm. saffron
¼ tsp. caraway seeds
Salt
Ghee

For the Mango Gravy:

6 large ripe mangoes of any type
   with golden flesh, skinned and
   cut both the cheeks each into 6
   pieces. You should get 36 pieces
1 cup coconut juice
1 large onion
8 Kashmiri chillies, deseeded
1 tbsp. aniseeds
1 tsp. cumin seeds   } Grind fine in a little water
1 tsp. coriander seeds
1 star anise
6 black peppercorns
½ cup fresh coriander,
   chopped
½ cup cashew nuts, halved and fried
½ cup washed, dried raisins and
   fried
2 sprigs curry leaves
Salt
Ghee

Preparation time	:	15 mins.
Cooking time	:	45 mins.
Serves	:	6

- Place the washed rice, fried onions, toasted crushed saffron, caraway seeds, salt and 2 tablespoons of ghee in an electric rice cooker and cook till tender.

- Meanwhile, place the finely ground masala and curry leaves in a large vessel along with 2 tablespoons of ghee. Put the vessel over a low heat and stir till it becomes red hot.

- Add the coconut milk and bring the masala to a boil. Add salt to taste and then the mangoes. Simmer for 5 minutes.

- Place ½ the saffron rice in a tapeli. Cover with the cooked mango gravy. Top with the rest of the rice. Decorate with the fried cashew nuts and raisins.

- Seal the mouth of the tapeli with foil, or a lid, bound with wheat dough. Place over an iron tava over medium heat for 15 minutes.

- Serve hot with fried chicken, sweet and sour mince and an onion kachumber.

CHOWLAI-NI-BHAJI

3 large bunches of chowlai bhaji
   leaves, plucked along with very
   tender stems
3 large onions, chopped fine
1½" crushed ginger
6 large garlic cloves, crushed
3 green chillies, deseeded and
   cut fine
2 tsps. broiled cumin seeds,
   coarsely ground
½ tsp. turmeric powder
Salt, Pure ghee

Preparation time	:	12-15 mins.
Cooking time	:	20 mins.
Serves	:	4-6

- Wash the bhaji leaves and stems twice and chop very fine.

- Place 3 tablespoons of ghee along with the onions in a vessel and allow to heat on a medium flame. When brown, put in the crushed ginger, garlic and cumin seeds. Lower the flame and stir for 2 minutes. Add the green chillies, bhaji leaves, turmeric and a little salt and cook gently for 7 minutes, stirring all the while. It should never be covered and allowed to get black.

- Serve with fried dried Bombay ducks, methia-nu-achar and rotlis.

KACCHI-KERI-NE-KOHRA-NU-DOHRU
(Raw Mango and Pumpkin Gravy)

400 gms. red pumpkin, skinned and
   cut into large chunks
4 small tender mangoes
2 large onions, chopped fine
4 green chillies ⎫
8 large garlic cloves ⎪
4 dried red chillies   Grind in
1 tbsp. cumin seeds ⎬ a little
3 black peppercorns   water
2 cardamom seeds ⎪
1 tsp. turmeric powder ⎭
½ cup crushed jaggery
½ cup finely chopped coriander
2 stalks curry leaves
Salt, Til (Sesame) Oil

Preparation time	:	8 mins.
Cooking time	:	25-30 mins.
Serves	:	6

- Boil the red pumpkin in 2 cups of water and a little salt and crush it to a pulp.

- Place the onions in a vessel, add 3 tbsps. of sesame oil and the curry leaves and chopped onions and cook them till soft and pink.

- Skin the mangoes, cut each into 2 pieces and discard the seeds.

- Add the ground masala to the onions and lower the flame and allow it to cook for 5 minutes. Add the raw mangoes and 1 cup of water and cook the mangoes till they are soft. Then add the crushed jaggery and the chopped coriander and allow to simmer for 7 minutes. Taste for salt and remove from the fire.

- Serve with khichri, fried fish and papads.

KACCHI-PAKKI-KERI-NO-PATIO

(Half-Ripened Mango Patio)

6-8 whole half-ripened mangoes of any type, if possible, get pairi mangoes, skinned and kept whole

2 large onions, chopped fine

½ fresh coconut, grated ⎤

6-8 green chillies, deseeded ⎥ Grind

8-10 large garlic cloves ⎥ fine in

1" fresh ginger root ⎥ a little

1½ tsp. cumin seeds ⎥ water

½ tsp. mustard seeds ⎦

3 large red tomatoes, skinned and chopped fine

1½ tsps. turmeric powder

2½ tsps. Cooverbai's dhansakh masala

2 sprigs curry leaves

Salt

Ghee or Sesame oil

- Put the chopped onions and curry sprigs along with ghee or oil, about 2½ tablespoons of oil into large vessel. Place on a medium heat and cook till golden brown.

- Add the ground masala and the turmeric and dhansakh powders, lower the heat and mix vigorously for 3 to 4 minutes. Add 2 cups of water and salt to taste and bring to a boil.

- When the mixture has boiled for 3 minutes, add the whole, skinned mangoes. Simmer on low heat for 10 minutes and remove from fire.

- Serve hot with white rice and yellow tuvar dal or with khichri and papads.

Preparation time	:	10 mins.
Cooking time	:	30 mins.
Serves	:	4-6

MEHERBAI WADIA-NU-BHUJELOO-ISTOO

(Meherbai Wadia's Baked Vegetable Stew)

8-10 eggs
300 gms. sliced onions
100 gms. frenchbeans, cut into
    fine slices
100 gms. carrots, cut into tiny cubes
100 gms. pumpkin, cut into tiny
    cubes
100 gms. sweet potatoes (ratalu),
    cut into tiny cubes
50 gms. boiled green peas
50 gms. ladyfingers, cut fine
15 gms. finely chopped ginger
15 gms. finely chopped garlic
4 large tomatoes, skinned and
    cut into slices
50 gms. thick cream
1 tbsp. chopped parsley
1 tbsp. sugar + 1 tbsp. white vinegar
½ tsp. nutmeg powder
Salt
Butter
Peanut oil

Preparation time	:	30 mins.
Cooking time	:	50 mins.
Serves	:	8

• Deep fry the sliced onions until a light golden brown and place in a sieve.

• In the same oil, fry each of the vegetables separately, and place in a large thali. Fry the green peas lightly and remove within 2 minutes.

• Poach the tomato slices in water, 1 tablespoon butter, 1 teaspoon sugar and a sprinkling of salt.

• Heat ½ tablespoon of butter and fry the ginger and garlic. Add the fried vegetables and the black pepper and nutmeg powders and mix gently. Add fine salt and the sugar and vinegar and mix again.

• Sprinkle the onion into the prepared vegetables and place into a pyrex dish.

• Place the poached tomato slices on top of the vegetables.

• Take a large flat-bottomed vessel or non-stick frying pan. Add a little water and salt. When it begins to boil, crack 3 eggs one at a time into it and poach them lightly. Place the poached eggs on the vegetables in the pyrex dish. Sprinkle with the parsley and place into an oven at 350⁰ C for 7 minutes.

• Serve with French bread or toast or rolls.

Dried Green Peas in Spinach (1)
Cooked Ripe Mangoes (2)
Black Eyed Beans Cooked
with Red Pumpkin (3)
Tomato Stuffed Rotlis (4)

SILLOO VAID-NI-DAHI-KADHI-MA-BHINDA

(Ladyfingers Cooked in Silloo Vaid's Curd Curry)

10 very large tender ladyfingers,
    each cut into 1" long pieces
500 gms. curd
2 onions, finely chopped
6 green chillies, deseeded ⎤
10 large cloves garlic   ⎬ Grind fine
1½ tsps. cumin seeds ⎦
2 tsps. sugar
4 tbsps. gram flour
1 tsp. red chilli powder
½ tsp. mustard seeds
½ cup finely chopped fresh
    coriander leaves
3 sprigs curry leaves
Salt
Peanut oil

Preparation time	:	10 mins.
Cooking time	:	20-25 mins.
Serves	:	4-6

- Place the chopped onions in an open mouthed vessel over medium heat along with 3 table-spoons of oil. When the oil get hot, add the mustard seeds and the curry leaves and allow the onions to become soft and pink in colour.

- Add the ground masala and the chilli powder and cook for 3 minutes over a low heat. Then add the gram flour and cook for 5 minutes, stirring non-stop. Then add 4 cups of water and mix the flour well so there are no lumps and allow the mixture to boil well. Add salt.

- Very lightly allow the ladyfinger pieces to roast in 4 teaspoons of oil. Stir up and down till still green and remove the pan from the fire.

- Whisk the curds. Lower the heat below the boiling water and add the curds and mix non-stop till the water and curds have become one. Taste for salt.

- Add the ladyfinger pieces to the curd curry and allow to simmer together for 7 minutes.

- Serve with vegetable khichri and ripe mango Bafenu pickle.

Dhansakh Dal with
Mangoes and Drumsticks (1)
Seasoned Yellow Toover Dal (2)
Prawns, Drumsticks, Raw Mango
and Pumpkin Gravy (3)

FARAJBEEJ-NA-TAAJA-DANA

(Fresh Frenchbean Seeds)

400 gms. fresh beans
  (frenchbean seeds)
250 gms. tomatoes, skinned
  and chopped fine
250 gms. onions, chopped fine
2 tsps. ginger-garlic masala
1 tsp. turmeric powder
2 tsps. red chilli powder
2 tsps. dhansakh masala
1 tsp. sugar
½ tsp. ajwain seeds
Salt
Peanut oil

Preparation time	:	10 mins.
Cooking time	:	40-45 mins.
Serves	:	4-6

- Place the onions in the pressure cooker along with 3 tablespoons of oil and cook till soft. Add the ginger-garlic paste and mix well.

- Wash the beans and add them to the onion mixture. Stir over a medium flame for 3 minutes. Then add the turmeric, chilli and dhansakh masala powders and salt and cook for 3 minutes.

- Add the tomatoes, ajwain seeds, sugar and water and cook till tender.

- Empty the contents of the cooker in a vessel. Place on a medium flame and evaporate the extra gravy till you get the desired consistency you want.

- Serve with dried fried Bombay Ducks and rotlis.

KHATTA-MITTHA-BHINDA

(Piquant Baby Ladyfingers)

500 gms. tender baby ladyfingers
2 tbsps. gram flour
2 Kashmiri chillies, broken into 2
2 tbsps. coconut, fresh grated
1 tbsp. fresh coriander, finely
  chopped
1 tsp. ground coriander
½ tsp. mustard seeds
1 pinch asafetida
1½ tsps. sugar
Salt
Peanut oil

Preparation time	:	7 mins.
Cooking time	:	20 mins.
Serves	:	4-6

- Wash and drain the water from the ladyfingers. Top and tail them and set aside.

- In a small thali, place the gram flour, coconut, coriander and sugar and crush it along with 2 teaspoons of oil.

- Heat ½ cup of oil and when hot, add the mustard seeds and asafetida and the dried broken chillies. Mix well and add the ladyfingers and stir for 2 minutes and lower the flame and cook for 7 minutes. Add the crushed gram and coconut flour mixture and keep stirring till it is all cooked. Sprinkle a little water and fine salt and lower from the flame when done.

PAPETA-NE-KHARI SING-NO-SUKKO-PATIO

(Patia made with Potatoes and Salted Peanuts)

500 gms. potatoes, skinned and
   chopped into ½" cubes
150 gms. salted crisp peanuts,
   crushed
2 onions, finely chopped
2 tomatoes, skinned and
   chopped
1½ tsps. cumin seeds   ⎤
6-8 cloves garlic   ⎦ Grind fine
1 tsp. turmeric powder
1 tsp. red chilli powder
1½ tsps. dhansakh masala
1 tsp. sambhar masala
2 curry sprigs
Salt, Sesame oil

- Soak the cubed potatoes in salted water for 20 minutes. Drain them and allow to dry. Heat a karahi, half filled with oil, and fry the potatoes in small batches till golden and soft. Set aside.

- Take same oil from the karahi, 3 tablespoons, and fry the curry sprigs and chopped onions till golden. Then add the tomatoes, stir for 2 minutes and put in the ground cumin and garlic and the 4 powdered masalas – turmeric, chilli, dhansakh and sambhar. Stir well and cook on a low fire, add a pinch of salt, stir and add the fried potatoes and simmer for 3 minutes. Add the crushed peanuts, stir and serve hot with wheat flour rotlis and prawn kababs.

Preparation time	:	12 mins.
Cooking time	:	35 mins.
Serves	:	4-6

KHATOO-MITTHOO-KOHRU

(Sweet and Sour Red Pumpkin)

500 gms. skinned red pumpkin,
   cut into small pieces
250 gms. onions, chopped fine
½ cup tamarind pulp
½ cup crushed jaggery
1½ tsps. broiled, coarsely
   ground cumin
1 tsp. turmeric powder
1½ tsps. red chilli powder
2 tsps. Parsi dhansakh masala
½ tsp. mustard seeds
2 sprigs curry leaves
Salt, Sesame oil

- Boil the pumpkin along with the salt, turmeric powder and 2 cups of water till soft. Crush it to a pulp.

- Place the curry leaves, onions, and mustard seeds in a vessel and cook till pink in 3 tablespoons of oil, over medium heat. Add the cumin, chilli powders and dhansakh masala, mix well, and add the tamarind and the jaggery. Lower the flame and add the pulped pumpkin. Taste for salt.

- Serve with a vegetable khichdi, papads and mango pickle in oil.

Preparation time	:	10 mins.
Cooking time	:	25 mins.
Serves	:	6-8

KHUS KHUSWALA-SOOKKA-LEELA-MARCHA-NA-PAPETA

(Potatoes with Poppy Seeds and Green Chillies)

750 gms. potatoes, skinned and
   chopped into 1" pieces
2 large onions, cut fine
4 large tomatoes, skinned and
   chopped
¼ cup mint leaves, chopped
½ cup coriander leaves, chopped
1½" ginger ⎤
6 large garlic cloves   Grind
8 Kashmiri chillies,   fine with
   deseeded   a little
2 tbsps. poppy seeds   water
1 tbsp. sesame seeds ⎦
½ tsp. mustard seeds
2 sprigs curry leaves
Salt
Sesame oil

Preparation time	:	15 mins.
Cooking time	:	35 mins.
Serves	:	4-6

- Place the cut potatoes into salted water.

- Place the chopped onions and curry leaves in a vessel with half a cup of oil and cook them till soft, stirring frequently. Add the potatoes and add 1 cup water and cover and cook till half done. Then add the ground masala and mix it well into the potatoes. Add the tomatoes along with another cup of water and cover and cook till tender. Taste for salt.

- Heat 2 teaspoons of oil in a small saucepan. Add the mustard seeds and allow to splutter and then put in the chopped green chillies and the coriander and cook for 2 minutes. Sprinkle this over the potatoes.

- Serve hot with wheat flour parathas and pani-nu-keri-nu-achar.

KATY DALAL-NU-KHARU-VENGNU-NE-PAPRI-NA-BEEJ

(Katy Dalal's Large Black Brinjals Cooked with Papri Beans)

1 very large black brinjal
350 gms. papri beans
2 large onions, finely chopped
1 bunch spring onions
1 bunch green garlic
2 tsps. ginger-garlic paste
5 large tomatoes, skinned and
    chopped fine
8 green chillies, deseeded and
    chopped
1½ tsps. turmeric or better still
1½" fresh turmeric, minced
1½ tsps. dhansakh masala
1 tsp. garam masala
2 tsps. sugar
2 sprigs curry leaves
Salt
Sesame oil

- Skin the brinjal, cut into long pieces and then thin, small pieces and soak them in salted water.

- Place the chopped onions and the chopped spring onions along with ½ cup of oil and the curry sprigs into a large vessel over a medium flame. Allow to cook till soft.

- To the onions add the finely chopped green garlic and the ginger-garlic paste and cook for 3 minutes. Then add the green chillies, turmeric, dhansakh masala and garam masala and allow to simmer for 5 minutes.

- Drain the brinjals from the water. Wash the papri beans twice, sprinkle a wee bit of salt on them and add them to the vessel along with the brinjal pieces. Stir and cook for 5 minutes so that the brinjals and beans are well coated with the masala.

- Then put the vessel's contents into a pressure cooker along with 2 cups of water and cook till the beans are tender. Empty the cooker's contents into a vessel. Taste for salt. If you have much gravy left, dry it up by allowing the vegetable and beans to simmer till dry. Sprinkle the sugar on the contents and stir till the sugar melts.

- Serve with hot rotlis and fried fish.

Preparation time	:	9 mins.
Cooking time	:	35-40 mins.
Serves	:	6-8

LAMBO-GHÉVRO

(Long Papri or Flat Beans)

450 gms. long ghévro papri, topped, tailed, cut into 3 pieces each

150 gms. sweet potatoes or ratalu kand, boiled and skinned

3 large onions, chopped fine

4 large tomatoes, skinned and chopped

½ cup crushed jaggery

20 garlic cloves, separated with skins on

3 tsps. Parsi dhansakh masala

2-3 tsps. chilli powder

1½ tsps. turmeric powder

½ tsp. ajwain seeds

Salt

Oil

Preparation time	:	15 mins.
Cooking time	:	35-40 mins.
Serves	:	4-6

- Wash the ghévro and allow the water to drain.

- Place the chopped onions along with 3 tablespoons of oil in a large kalai patia over medium heat and allow to cook till golden in colour. Add the large unskinned cloves of garlic and the ajwain seeds and cook for 2 minutes before adding the turmeric and chilli powders. Mix well for 2 minutes and add the ghévro and lower the flame and stir well. Add salt and the tomatoes and cover and cook for 7 minutes. Then add 2 cups of water and allow to simmer till soft and done. Place some water on the lid and if the water in the tapeli dries up, add the water on the lid.

- Whilst the ghévro is cooking, boil water in a large vessel. Wash the sweet potatoes, slice them thickly, and boil in the hot water. Remove from the water, skin and set aside.

- When the vegetables are almost cooked, sprinkle over the Parsi dhansakh masala and the crushed jaggery. Mix well. Add the boiled sweet potatoes and sprinkle some hot water, about half a cup over the vegetables. Mix again and simmer for 5 more minutes before removing from the stove.

- Serve hot with wheat rotlis and mutton kababs or cutlets.

MOTTA-BHARELA-PAPETA

(Large Stuffed Potatoes)

6 very large potatoes, all one size
    and shape
150 gms. fresh double beans
1 large onion
4 large tomatoes
2 tbsps. finely ground coconut
½ tsp. turmeric powder
½ tsp. red chilli powder
½ tsp. garam masala
2 tbsps. chopped coriander leaves
¼ tsp. black mustard seeds
10 curry leaves
Salt
Peanut oil

Preparation time	:	10 mins.
Cooking time	:	45-55 mins.
Serves	:	6-8

• Place the potatoes after washing them into a large tapeli and boil them till they are ¾ cooked. Gently remove them from the water and skin them and allow them to cool.

• In the meantime, heat 2 tablespoons of oil in a medium sized tapeli and add the onions, curry leaves and mustard seeds and cook till the onions are soft and pink. Then add the ground coconut, stir for 2 minutes and add the turmeric, chilli and garam masala powders. Mix for 3 minutes and add the double beans and cook for another 3 minutes. Add 2 cups of water, cover and allow to simmer for 10 minutes. Add the tomatoes and chopped coriander leaves and another cup of water and cook on simmer till the beans are soft. Do not cook in the pressure cooker as the beans will become mushy. The bean mixture should be tender and dry. Taste for salt.

• Skin the cold potatoes and cut them vertically into 2 pieces. Scoop out the centers of both pieces. Then pile the beans onto one side of the potato and cover with the other. Tie both the pieces together with a thin white string.

• Lightly salt the potatoes and fry them 2 or 3 at a time in a large flat-bottomed frying pan till golden and red on both sides.

• Serve along with the strings. Tomato or tamarind and date sauce would be an ideal accompaniment.

VATANA-SOORAN-KOTHMIR-NI-TARKARI

4 large onions, finely chopped
500 gms. shelled peas
250 gms. sooran, cut into ½" cubes
150 gms. carrots, cut into ½" cubes
2 bunches coriander leaves only
1 tbsp. crushed garlic
1 tbsp. finely chopped ginger
4 large tomatoes, skinned and
  finely chopped
6 Kashmiri chillies, deseeded ⎤
10 black peppercorns   ⎟ Grind
1 tbsp. broiled cumin seeds   ⎟ in a
1 tbsp. broiled coriander seeds ⎬ little
1 tbsp. broiled sesame seeds ⎟ water
½ tsp. mustard seeds   ⎟
1 tsp. turmeric powder   ⎦
2 sprigs curry leaves
Salt
Peanut oil

Preparation time	:	15-20 mins.
Cooking time	:	40-45 mins.
Serves	:	6-10

- Wash the peas and parboil them in salted water.

- Wash the sooran pieces and set aside. Do the same to the carrots.

- Wash the coriander leaves and chop finely.

- Heat a karahi with oil. It should be half full and place on medium heat. When hot, lower the flame and fry the sooran pieces. Remove when soft from the oil and fry the carrot pieces till soft. Remove, drain in a colander and set both vegetables aside.

- Place 2 tablespoons of oil from the karahi into a tapeli, add the chopped onions, garlic and ginger and curry sprigs and cook till golden red. Add the turmeric and ground masala and lower the heat and cook for 3 minutes. Then add the parboiled green peas and tomatoes and some salt and allow to simmer for 10 minutes by which time, the green peas should be soft. If they are still hard, add 1 cup of water, cover and simmer till they are done.

- Add the chopped coriander leaves and the fried sooran and carrots and ½ cup of water. Taste for salt. Simmer for another 7 minutes.

- Serve hot along with mutton cutlets or patties and lime pickle.

LEELI-KERI-PAPETA-NE-SING-MA

(Raw Mangoes Cooked with Potatoes and Drumsticks)

4 raw mangoes, tender skinned and
    chopped into ½" pieces
6 large potatoes, skinned and
    chopped into 1" squares and
    washed
4 drumsticks, cleaned and each cut
    into 4 pieces
6 Kashmiri chillies, deseeded ⎤
4 green chillies, deseeded |
1 tsp. turmeric powder | Grind
10 black peppercorns | fine in
1 tbsp. broiled cumin seeds   } a little
1 tbsp. broiled coriander seeds | water
1 tbsp. broiled sesame seeds |
1 tbsp. chopped garlic |
1½ tbsp. chopped ginger |
8 curry leaves   ⎦
Salt
Pure ghee

Preparation time	:	12 mins.
Cooking time	:	30-35 mins.
Serves	:	6

- Place the drumsticks in a pan of salted water and cook them till soft. Drain and set aside.

- Boil the mango pieces in 2 cups of water with a pinch of salt and set aside when tender.

- Place 2 tablespoons of ghee and the curry leaves in a medium sized vessel on a low flame. When the ghee heats up, add the masala and fry for 3 minutes till red. Then add the potatoes and stir well for 3 minutes. When they are well-coated with the masala, add 2 cups of water and allow to simmer for 15 to 20 minutes, till soft and tender. If necessary, add a little extra water.

- Remove the mango pieces and the drumstick pieces from the water in which they were boiled and add to the cooked potatoes. Stir well and allow to simmer for 5 more minutes.

- Serve hot with wheat rotlis and a dry fish dish.

LEELI-KACCHI-KERI-NE-LAL KOHRA-NO-KHIMO
(Green Mangoes Minced and Cooked with Red Pumpkin)

4 green tender mangoes, skinned
    and chopped into ½" square
    pieces, finely minced with a knife
300 gms. red pumpkin, cut into
    ½" square pieces
4 spring onions, cut julienne
1½" fresh ginger sliced thinly
    and cut julienne
5-6 green chillies, cut julienne,
    deseeded
1½" fresh turmeric, finely minced
1½ tbsps. fresh coriander, finely
    chopped
Salt
Pure ghee

- Place 3 tablespoons of ghee in a langri over a medium flame. When hot, add the curry leaves and green chillies and after 2 minutes, add the spring onions, cut into very thin slices.

- Mix lightly for 3 minutes and then add the ginger and fresh turmeric. Stir lightly for 2 minutes and add the pumpkin pieces and fine salt. Cover and allow to simmer over a low flame. Sprinkle some water. Simmer until the flesh is soft. Sprinkle the raw mango mince and stir gently. Add ½ cup of water, cover and cook till dry. Remove from the pan and cover with the chopped coriander.

- Serve with hot masoor dal khichri, papad and green coriander and coconut chutney.

Preparation time	:	10 mins.
Cooking time	:	15 mins.
Serves	:	4-6

TAJAA-DOUBLE BEEJ-NARIEL-MA
(Fresh Double Beans Cooked with Coconut)

400 gms. fresh double beans,
    removed from their pods
1 coconut, milk removed
1 tsp. black pepper powder
1 tsp. turmeric powder
1 tsp. red chilli powder
½ tsp. caraway seeds
2 cups tomato puree
2 tsps. sugar
Salt
2 tbsps. butter – preferably white

- Wash the double beans and cook them in water. Add some salt and boil till tender. Set aside. Do not cook in a pressure cooker.

- Place the coconut milk in a heavy-bottomed pan and place on a very slow fire. Add the boiled double beans and throw away the water. Sprinkle the black pepper, turmeric and chilli powders onto the beans. Crush the caraway seeds between your palms and add them also and allow to simmer till the milk thickens. Then add the puree, sugar and butter and simmer for some more time till the double beans are in a thick sauce. Taste for salt and remove from the fire.

Preparation time	:	18 mins.
Cooking time	:	50 mins. to
		1 Hour
Serves	:	4-6

- Serve hot with brun pau and fish cutlets.

KAWLA-BHINDA-TAMBOTA-NA-RAS-MA

(Baby Ladyfingers Cooked in Tomato Gravy)

200 gms. very tender baby ladyfingers
400 gms. large red tomatoes, skinned
2 medium sized onions, chopped fine
6 red Kashmiri chillies, deseeded ⎤
8 large cloves garlic ⎟ Grind fine with a little water
1 tsp. cumin seeds, broiled ⎟
1 tsp. coriander seeds, broiled ⎦
½ tsp. black mustard seeds
2 split green chillies, deseeded
Large pinch of sugar
Salt
Sunflower oil

Preparation time	:	10 mins.
Cooking time	:	20 mins.
Serves	:	4-6

Wash the ladyfingers, allow to dry and then top and tail them and set aside. Sprinkle a little fine salt on them.

- Place the finely chopped onions in a medium sized langri with 2 tablespoons of oil and cook till soft and pink.

- Puree the tomatoes and add them to the cooked onions on the fire, then add the ground masala and mix well and allow to simmer for 7 minutes. If necessary, add ½ cup of water. Taste for salt.

- Deep fry the whole ladyfingers in a frying pan in 3 small batches and shake off the oil and add them to the hot gravy on the fire.

- Heat 1 tablespoon of oil and add the mustard seeds and allow them to crackle, and sprinkle over the cooked ladyfingers in the gravy. Remove from the fire and serve hot.

- Eat with parathas and fried fish.

MASALA-NI-GOVARSING

(Masala Cooked Govarsing)

400 gms. govarsing, very tender, topped and tailed

8 Kashmiri chillies ⎤
1 tbsp. jeera ⎥ Grind
8 large garlic cloves ⎥ well in
1 tbsp. turmeric powder ⎬ little
2 tsps. chilli powder ⎥ water
2 tsps. sambhar powder ⎦

½ cup crushed jaggery ⎤ Mix well
½ cup tamarind pulp ⎦

2 onions ⎤
2 green chillies ⎥ Grind
½ bunch coriander leaves ⎬ well
7 peppercorns ⎥
1 1" piece cinnamon ⎦

Salt
Sesame oil

Preparation time	:	20 mins.
Cooking time	:	30-35 mins.
Serves	:	6

- Wash the govarsing well and then boil it in a little salted water till soft. Discard the water – it will be slightly bitter.

- Place the ground chilli and onion masala in a vessel with 3 tablespoons of oil. Cook till the masala has boiled well and then add the Kashmiri chilli ground masala. Lower the flame and allow masala to simmer for 3 minutes. Stir in the govarsing and taste for salt. Simmer for 5 to 7 minutes.

- Serve hot with rice rotlis and Parsi pora (omelette).

KESARI KHICHRI

(Khichdi Cooked With Saffron)

For the Rice:

400 gms. basmati rice
150 gms. masoor dal
½ tsp. turmeric
1 gm. saffron
2-3 deep fried onions
8 black peppercorns
Milk from 1½ coconuts
3 cloves
3 crushed green cardamoms
1" piece cinnamon
3 bay leaves
Salt
Pure ghee

For pouring over the Rice:

1 bunch spring onions, cut upto
   6" above the roots
4 green chillies, deseeded and
   finely chopped
1 tsp. minced garlic
1 tsp. minced ginger
½ cup freshly chopped coriander
20 almonds in their skins, lightly
   fried
20 cashew nuts, lightly fried
¼ cup seedless raisins, lightly fried
Salt
Pure ghee

Preparation time	:	15 mins.
Cooking time	:	55-65 mins.
Serves	:	4

- Wash the rice and place it in a rice cooker along with the washed masoor dal. Add the turmeric, fried onions, peppercorns, cloves, cardamoms, cinnamon piece, bay leaves and the coconut milk along with the salt. Heat the saffron with great care on a tava by pushing it up and down with a wadded piece of muslin. Do not blacken and add it to the cooker. Check that your coconut milk is in sufficient quantity to cook your rice. Cook till rice is soft and aromatic. When cooked, keep it in the cooker for 5 minutes and then empty it into a large vessel.

- Chop the spring onions very fine and place them in a frying pan along with 2 tablespoons of ghee. Add the green chillies, ginger and garlic, a pinch of salt and cook till soft. Add the fried whole almonds, cashew nuts and raisins and mix into the khichdi. Cover with a tight lid.

- Place the vessel on a tava over medium heat for 20 minutes before eating it.

- Serve with sweet or sour dahi or a sweet and sour mince gravy and green salad.

GARAM-CHAVAL-NE-THANDOO-DAHI

(Warm Rice with Cold Curds)

Sometimes after a heavy meal, you long for some light food. Dahi and chaas or buttermilk is always available at all farms, at all times. Everyday, milk was turned into dahi and then churned into butter, which is made into pure ghee.

1 kg. Basmati rice
4 green cardamoms, lightly crushed
Salt
Pure ghee
2 kg. creamy curds, whisked with
    ½ cup sugar
8 green chillies, slit and deseeded
1½" ginger, sliced and cut julienne
3 large tomatoes, skinned and thinly
    sliced
½ cup raisins, washed and fried
100 gms. almonds, sliced and fried
100 gms. pistachios, sliced and fried
2 sprigs curry leaves
Pure ghee

Preparation time	:	8-10 mins.
Cooking time	:	40-45 mins.
Serves	:	8-10

- Cook the rice in a rice cooker along with the green cardamoms, salt and ½ cup of pure ghee and sufficient water.

- Whisk the cold dahi with salt.

- Take a large tapeli. Put in ½ cup of pure ghee and place on medium heat. When the ghee smokes, add the green chillies and tomatoes and salt. Then remove the vessel immediately from the fire. Cool and add to the cold curd and stir vigorously.

- Top with fried raisins, almond and pistachio slices.

- Serve with hot rice and papads.

KATY DALAL-NI-MASALAMA-TARKARI-NI-KHICHRI

(Katy Dalal's Masala Vegetable Khichdi)

For the Rice:

400 gms. basmati rice
150 gms. masoor dal
2 deep fried onions
1 tsp. turmeric powder
3-5 spice leaves, fresh or dry
2 one inch pieces cinnamon
3 green cardamoms, crushed
Salt
2 tbsps. pure ghee

For the Vegetables:

1 gm. saffron
2 onions, finely chopped
4 large tomatoes, skinned and
    chopped fine
100 gms. potatoes, skinned and
    cut into ½" cubes
100 gms. carrots, skinned and
    cut into ½" cubes
100 gms. red pumpkin, skinned
    and cut into ½" cubes
100 gms. sweet potato, skinned
    and cut into ½" cubes
100 gms. purple yam or kamodio
    kand, skinned and cut into
    ½" cubes
50 gms. frenchbeans, cut fine
50 gms. fried ladyfingers
100 gms. fried raisins, seedless⎤ Keep
50 gms. fried cashew nuts   ⎦ aside
1 tsp. turmeric powder
1½ tsps. chilli powder
1½ tsps. garam masala
2 green chillies
Salt
Pure ghee

- Prepare the rice in a rice cooker along with the ingredients written for the rice.

- Take a large, open-mouthed vessel with a thick bottom. Cook the onions in it in ½ cup of pure ghee over a low fire. When the onions turn pink wash all the vegetables, except the ladyfingers, and salt them lightly and add to the pan along with the turmeric powder and chillies. Stir well for 5 minutes and then add the tomatoes, salt and the chilli powder and cover and cook over a very low fire for 5 minutes. Then add 1 cup water, cover and put water on the lid and allow to simmer till tender. Keep adding more hot water from the lid as you need it. When the vegetables are cooked, sprinkle the garam masala on top. Simmer till tight. Taste for salt.

- Heat the saffron on an iron tava and crumble it between your fingers and then sprinkle it on top of the vegetables and stir thoroughly.

- Put half the rice in a large vessel and pour all the vegetables on top of it. Then cover it with the remaining half of the rice. Decorate with the fried ladyfingers, raisins and cashew nuts. Cover tightly and place over a tava on medium flame for 20 minutes.

- Serve in a flat dish along with sweet dahi, fried prawns and green salad.

Preparation time	:	15 mins.
Cooking time	:	1 hr.
Serves	:	6-8

TAMBOTA-NI-ROTLI
(Tomato Stuffed Rotlis)

For the Covering:

1 cup wheat flour
1 cup self-raising flour
¼ tsp. crushed ajwain
1 tbsp. coriander, finely chopped
Salt
Ghee

For the Stuffing:

1 small white sweet onion, chopped
   very fine
1 green chilli, chopped very fine
3 large tomatoes, skinned,
   deseeded, and chopped very fine
1 large pinch of sugar
¼ tsp. turmeric powder
½ tsp. red chilli powder
½ tsp. black pepper powder
½ tsp. ginger-garlic paste
3 stalks curry leaves, finely chopped
Salt
Ghee

Preparation time	:	25 mins.
Cooking time	:	25 mins.
Serves	:	6

- Place the flours, ajwain and salt in a thali. Mix well and add the ghee and sufficient water to make a supple dough. Knead well till smooth. Cover with a damp cloth and keep aside for 2 hours.

- Take 1 tablespoon of pure ghee and the curry leaves and place it on a very low fire. Keep stirring for 3 minutes and then add the ginger-garlic paste, turmeric, red chilli and black pepper powders. Mix for 2 minutes and then add the chopped green chilli and tomatoes, along with the sugar. Allow to simmer until the mixture thickens. Add salt and stir.

- Roll the dough into 12 to 14 round rotlis.

- Take half the rotlis and divide the mixture between them, taking care to keep a clear ½" margin around the paste and the circumference of the rotli. Apply water around the clear edges and cover the rotli with another one. Pat the edges so the rotlis stick together.

- When all your double rotlis are ready, place an iron tava on the fire. When it gets hot, rub it with a soft cloth and place the stuffed rotli onto the hot surface. Turn it once and then again and apply a trickle of ghee around the edges. Turn over once again until both sides are golden and brown.

- Serve as a breakfast or tea-time snack with hot elaichi tea.

Masala Cooked Govarsing (1)
Masala Gherkins (2)
Bitter Bean Dal (Val-ni-Dal) (3)
Curd Relish (4)

184

dals

SADI-MAG-NI-DAL
(Simple Moong Dal)

400 gms. moong dal, washed twice
1½" amba halad, finely minced
6 large cloves garlic, sliced
3 green chillies, deseeded and
   minced
¼ cup chopped fresh coriander
½ tsp. turmeric powder
¼ tsp. mustard seeds
¼ tsp. cumin seeds
Salt
Pure ghee

Preparation time	:	5 mins.
Cooking time	:	22 mins.
Serves	:	4-6

- Place the washed moong dal in a kalai tapeli and add water and salt and place on medium heat. Do not cook in a pressure cooker as it will turn to mush. Add the turmeric powder. Remove the slush which will float on top of the dal.

- Cook the dal till it is soft with at least ½ cup of liquid left.

- Heat 2 tablespoons of pure ghee in a small karahi over slow heat. When the ghee heats up, add the amba halad and green chillies and mix for 2 minutes and then add the cumin and mustard seeds and allow them to crackle. Then mix in the fresh coriander and pour the waghar onto the dal.

- Mix and serve with fresh ladi pau for breakfast or lunch.

MASALA-NI-VAAL-NI DAL
(Bitter Bean Dal)

350 gms. vaal dal, washed twice
2 medium sized onions, chopped
1 tsp. turmeric powder
2 tsps. red chilli powder
3 tbsps. fresh ground coconut
1 tbsp. sugar
Salt
Sesame oil

Preparation time	:	7 mins.
Cooking time	:	40 mins.
Serves	:	4

- Chop the onions and place in a tapeli with 3 tablespoons of oil. Cook over a medium flame till pink in colour. Add the coconut, turmeric and chilli powders and cook for 3 minutes, stirring all the while. Add the washed dal and stir well for 3 more minutes.

- Lower the flame and add 3 cups water, cover and simmer over a low fire till cooked. The beans should remain intact and soft. They should not be mushy and disintegrated.

- Serve with fried or roasted dry Bombay Ducks and rice rotlis.

VAGHARELI-MORI-DAL

(Seasoned Yellow Toover Dal)

400 gms. toover dal
1 tsp. turmeric powder
Salt
Pure ghee

For the Vaghar:

6 green chillies, slit into 4,
   deseeded and cut into large
   pieces
½ cup freshly chopped coriander
6 large mint leaves
6 curry leaves, chopped into 2
8 large garlic cloves, thinly sliced
2 onions, sliced and deep fried in oil
½ tsp. coarsely crushed cumin
   seeds
¼ tsp. coarsely crushed coriander
   seeds
¼ tsp. nigella or onion seeds
2 sprigs, whole fresh coriander for
   decoration
Salt
Pure ghee

Preparation time	:	10 mins.
Cooking time	:	30-35 mins.
Serves	:	6

- Soak the dal for ½ hour. Wash twice and place in a pressure cooker with 4 to 5 cups of water, salt and 2 tablespoons of pure ghee. Cook till soft.

- Pass the dal through a moulee legume or any other fine sieve and place in a tapeli.

- Take a medium sized karahi. Add 2 tablespoons of pure ghee and when hot, put in the garlic slices, chilli pieces, cumin, coriander and nigella seeds, as well as the curry leaves. Stir vigorously for 3 minutes and remove from the fire.

- Place the sieved dal over a low flame and allow to simmer. Taste for salt.

- To serve, place the hot dal in individual bowls. Top each bowl with the deep fried onions and then top it again with the fried garlic, chilli, curry leaves and the cumin, coriander and nigella seeds. Sprinkle with the freshly chopped coriander and mint leaves. If serving in a large bowl or dish, add the herbs and spices in the center of the bowl and decorate with the coriander sprigs. Fresh, whole red chillies look exceptionally good.

- Serve with gutlis or parathas or rotlis for breakfast or lunch.

- In our house, this particular dal is served with hot, fried, fresh Bombay Ducks and lots of sour lime pieces.

KHATTA-MITTHA-KABULI-CHANA

(Sweet and Sour Chick Peas)

250 gms. chick peas
1 onion, finely chopped
2 tomatoes, finely chopped
4 boiled potatoes, finely chopped
1 tbsp. chilli powder
1 tbsp. cumin powder
1 tbsp. coriander powder
1 tbsp. garam masala powder
½ cup coriander, finely chopped
½ cup tamarind pulp   ⎤ Mix and
½ cup crushed jaggery   ⎦ melt well
Salt
Oil

Preparation time	:	15 mins.
Cooking time	:	45 mins.
Serves	:	6

- Soak the chick peas overnight. They will swell almost double in size. Next morning, wash them well and cook along with water and salt in a pressure cooker till soft, but intact.

- Put the onions in a large vessel and cook over a medium flame in 2 tablespoons of oil till soft.

- Add the chilli, cumin and coriander powders as well as the garam masala. Mix for 2 minutes and add the tomatoes. Lower the flame and cook till you get a nice, thick mixture. Add the chick peas after draining them from the water in which they were boiled. Mix well and add the boiled potatoes, coriander and tamarind-jaggery pulp. Allow to simmer for 5 minutes.

- Serve hot with parathas and a mango pickle in oil.

TAMBOTA-MA-CHORA

(Black-Eyed Beans cooked in Tomato Puree)

300 gms. black-eyed beans, soaked
   overnight in water
2 large onions
5 large tomatoes, skinned,
   deseeded, pulped
2 capsicums, cut julienne and
   lightly fried
1 tbsp. cumin powder
1 tbsp. coriander powder
1 tsp. red chilli powder
1 tbsp. garlic pulp
1 tbsp. sugar
Salt
Sunflower oil

Preparation time	:	15 mins.
Cooking time	:	35-40 mins.
Serves	:	6

- Wash the black-eyed beans twice and cook in salted water in a pressure cooker till tender.

- Place the onions in a tapeli along with 2 tablespoons of ghee over a low fire.

- When the onion softens, add the pulped garlic and stir for 2 minutes. Then add the cumin, coriander, red chilli powders. Stir well for 3 minutes before adding the sugar and the pulped tomatoes. Add salt and cook till it thickens. Remove from the fire.

- Drain the beans and add them to the tomato pulp and allow to simmer for 7 minutes until the gravy is thick.

- Serve hot in a round dish, with the capsicums sprinkled on top. To be eaten with peti pau.

PANCH-JATNI-DAL-KHATTI-MITTHI

(5 Different Dals, sweet & sour, all cooked together)

100 gms. tuvar dal
100 gms. masoor dal
100 gms. mung dal   } Soak them in water for 2 hours
100 gms. chana dal
100 gms. urad dal
4 large onions, finely chopped
1½ tbsps. Parsi dhansakh masala
2 tsps. red chilli powder
1½ tsps. turmeric powder
1 tsp. cumin powder
1 tsp. fennel powder
1 tsp. cinnamon powder
1 tsp. black peppercorn powder
½ cup tamarind pulp
½ cup crushed jaggery   } Mix well
6 green chillies, deseeded and cut
    fine
8 large clovers garlic, sliced
2 sprig curry leaves
Salt
Ghee

Preparation time	:	7 mins.
Cooking time	:	35 mins.
Serves	:	4-6

- Cook the 4 onions in 3 tablespoons of ghee and sufficient water in the pressure cooker. When soft and pink, add the curry leaves and cook for 1 minute.

- Add all the powdered masalas to the soft onions and stir briskly for 3 minutes. Then add the dals, all drained and washed twice. Add salt and sufficient amount of water and cook till tender.

- Remove the cooked dals into a tapeli, add the tamarind and jaggery pulp and allow to simmer for 7 minutes.

- Take a small karahi. Place on a low fire and add 1 tablespoon of ghee. When it becomes hot, add the garlic slices and stir till they become red. Add the green chillies, stir for 1 minute and remove the karahi from the flames.

- Remove the hot dals into a deep dish or tureen and top with the fried garlic, chillies and ghee.

- Serve with peti pau and dried Bombay Ducks, roasted or fried, along with plenty of onion kachumber.

SAFED-SOOKKA-VATANA-NE-VENGNU

(Dried White Peas cooked with Brinjals)

300 gms. dried white peas
250 gms. black brinjals, cut into
   1" pieces
1 onion, finely chopped
4 spring onions, finely chopped
4 green chillies, deseeded and
   finely chopped
1 cup large methi bhaji, leaves only,
   finely chopped
4 large tomatoes, skinned and finely
   chopped
6 red chillies
1 tbsp. cumin seeds
1 tbsp. coriander seeds   Grind fine
8 large garlic cloves   with a
1½ tsps. turmeric powder   little
2 tbsps. dry kopra, grated   water
1 1" piece cinnamon
6 black peppercorns
Salt
Sunflower oil

Preparation time	:	12 mins.
Cooking time	:	45 mins.
Serves	:	4-6

• Soak the peas overnight in a tapeli of water. Next day, cook the peas in salted water in a pressure cooker.

• Place the finely chopped onion and spring onions in a patia. Add 3 tablespoons oil and place on medium heat and cook till pink and soft.

• Wash the brinjals and large methi bhaji and cut them and keep aside. Keep the tomatoes chopped and ready.

• Add the finely ground masala to the onions, lower the flame and cook for 2 minutes until red and then add the brinjals and the large methi bhaji and stir well. Add salt lightly and put in the tomatoes, mix and cover and cook for 7 minutes. Place water on the lid. Add the water when it becomes hot into the patia, and mix and cook till soft. If the brinjal does not soften easily, don't worry. Add the boiled peas along with as much of its soup as necessary and allow to simmer for 10 minutes. The gravy should be thick. Taste for salt.

• Serve very hot, along with coconut chutney, mango pickle, fried or dried Bombay Ducks and wheat or rice rotlis.

CHORA-LAL-KOHRA-SAATHE-RANDHELA

(Black-Eyed Beans cooked with Red Pumpkin)

400 gms. chora or black-eyed beans, soaked overnight
300 gms. red pumpkin, skinned and cut into 1" squares
700 gms. large tomatoes, finely chopped
3 large onions, finely chopped
1 tbsp. ginger-garlic paste
1 tbsp. cinnamon-clove-black pepper powder
1 tbsp. red chilli powder
1 tbsp. Kairi sambhar
1½ tsps. turmeric powder
½ cup coriander, finely chopped
Salt
Pure Ghee or Peanut oil

Preparation time	:	7 mins.
Cooking time	:	45 mins.
Serves	:	6-8

• Wash the soaked beans twice and cook them in the pressure cooker along with salt, turmeric powder and the ginger-garlic paste.

• Place a large vessel on the stove at the same time. Add the onions and 3 tablespoons of ghee and cook over a medium flame. When the onion turns golden brown, add the spice powder, chilli powder and Kairi sambhar powder and stir well for 2 minutes. Then add the tomatoes and allow to simmer for 5 minutes over a low fire. Add the pumpkin pieces and salt and mix well. Add 1 cup of water. Cover and cook till soft.

• As soon as the choras are cooked, add them along with their soup to the cooked pumpkin pieces. Stir in gently and simmer over a low fire for 7 to 10 minutes. Mix in the fresh coriander and serve hot.

• Accompany with fried, fresh fish and bread slices or rotlis.

Chutney / Pickles

TAMBOTA-APPLE-KISMIS-NE-KHAJOOR-NI-CHUTNEY

(Tomato-Apple-Raisin and Date Chutney)

1500 gms. tomatoes
500 gms. apples
200 gms. seedless raisins, washed
200 gms. seeded and chopped dates
550 gms. sugar
150 gms. crushed jaggery
20 gms. ginger (amba halad), sliced,
   then cut into fine strips
15 gms. large garlic cloves, sliced
   and cut into strips and dried
6 Kashmiri chillies, ground in
   3 tsps. of sugarcane vinegar
1 tsp. turmeric
2 tsps. ground cinnamon-cloves-
   black peppercorns
1½ cup sugarcane vinegar
2 sprigs curry leaves
Salt

- Cut X marks on the bottoms of the tomatoes. Pour boiling water over them and allow them to stay in the water for 3 minutes. Drain the water, skin them and chop fine.

- Peel, core and chop the apples into small pieces.

- Place the cut tomatoes, apples and sugar in a large pan and allow to cook over medium heat till the mixture is thick and sticky. Taste for salt.

- Add the jaggery, amba halad, garlic, chillies, turmeric, spice powder, vinegar and curry leaves.

- Simmer for 10 minutes and remove from the heat.

- Cool and store in clean jars.

Preparation time	:	20 mins.
Cooking time	:	1 Hour
Serves	:	20

KERI-NE-JERDALOO-NI-CHUTNEY

(Raw Mango and Apricot Chutney)

1400 gms. skinned tender mangoes,
   cut into 1" pieces
1600 gms. sugar
300 gms. apricots, soaked in vinegar
   and sugar overnight
100 gms. dried sliced garlic
100 gms. dried sliced ginger
1 tbsp. Kashmiri chilli powder
1½ tbsps. garam masala powder
Coarse Salt

- Slowly cook the mangoes till soft and tender in 4 cups of water. When they have softened, add the sugar and cook till you get a good syrup. Cook till the syrup becomes sticky. Then add the dried garlic and ginger, stir and add the soaked apricots and the seedless raisins and simmer over a low fire for 10 minutes.

- Once the mangoes are ready, add the salt, chilli powder and garam masala and simmer for 5 minutes and remove from the heat.

- Store in the refrigerator.

Preparation time	:	20 mins.
Cooking time	:	40-50 mins.
Serves	:	20

KOHRA-NU-ACHAAR
(Pumpkin Pickle)

When you have very large pumpkins growing on your roof or in your garden, it becomes a problem for you. What do you do with 4 Kgs. to 20 Kgs. pumpkin at one go?

What I did was sit down to make some pickles, chutneys and jams that would last me through the year, as well as be helpful in giving them as gifts. Here are a few of my recipes which you can make use of. Always taste the product before removing it from the fire.

400 gms. red pumpkin, skinned and chopped into ½" pieces
275 gms. sugar
2-3 cups vinegar
½ cup crushed jaggery
100 gms. dried apricots, soaked overnight in sugar water
100 gms. red raisins, soaked overnight in sugar water
1 tsp. red Kashmiri chilli powder
½ tsp. dried ginger powder
2½ tsps. powdered black peppercorns, cinnamon, cloves, cardamoms and star anise
Coarse Salt

Preparation time	:	10 mins.
Cooking time	:	40-50 mins.
Serves	:	15-20

• Skin and chop the pumpkin into ½" pieces and place them in a large vessel. Not an aluminium one please. Sprinkle over with the sugar and allow to keep for 4 hours. Crush the jaggery and add it to the pumpkin.

• After 4 hours, during which time the sugar should have melted, place the vessel on a low fire. Add the apricots and raisins. Mix until the sugar has melted completely and then add coarse salt to taste and 2 cups of vinegar. Increase the heat and allow the mixture to boil. Taste. If you feel more vinegar is necessary, add ½ cup at a time. Place a teaspoon of your syrup in a saucer and touch it with your finger. If it is sticky, the pickle is ready.

• Add the chilli powder, ginger powder and the garam masala powder. Mix for 3 minutes and remove from the fire.

• This pickle can be eaten immediately.

PRAKASH'S GARAM MASALA

...n has been working for me for the last 23 years and has become an expert on ...i food. He has experimented with different spices and one of the best mixes is given below:

100 gms. Cinnamon
50 gms. Cloves
5 whole Green Cardamom seeds
25 gms. Variali
20 gms. Cumin seeds
10 gms. Mace
25 gms. Star Anise
10 gms. Shahjeera seeds
10 gms. Big Brown Cardamoms

- Broil the above spices lightly over an iron tava. Cool. Grind very fine. Bottle tightly. Use in meat dishes and pulaos.

ALLAMAI KATRAK-NO-DHANA-JEERA-NO-MASALO

3 kgs. broiled dhania
¾ kg. broiled cumin
100 gms. broiled turmeric pieces
100 gms. broiled badiyan
100 gms. broiled sesame seeds
100 gms. broiled mustard seeds
100 gms. broiled poppy seeds
100 gms. broiled Ram patti
100 gms. broiled large black (elcha)
    cardamoms
100 gms. chinkabab
100 gms. nagkesar
100 gms. broiled shahjeera
100 gms. broiled mace (javintri)
100 gms. broiled Kashmiri red
    chillies
100 gms. broiled cinnamon
100 gms. broiled bay leaves
    (tamal patta)
50 gms. cloves
2 nutmeg (jaiphal)

- Grind the above masala very fine. Pass through a fine sieve. Store in dry large glass bottles and keep in a cool, dark place.

HOW TO MAKE PURE GHEE

1 kg. cream
2 betel nut leaves

- Place the betel nut leaves and the crea[m] thick bottomed vessel, preferably a kalai pa[n] langri.

- Put the vessel over medium heat. The cream will heat and melt and turn into ghee. Do not disturb the boiling process by stirring the liquid with a spoon. The portion that is not needed will stick to the bottom and become brown or red. Lower the flame and cook till clear ghee floats above the fuzz.

- Strain the liquid through a fine sieve into a clean glass jar. Discard the leaves.

- Place water in the vessel to soak the fuzz before washing it.

- Since the cream is very expensive, you could collect it from your daily home quota. Heat your fresh milk, cool it and chill it overnight. The next morning you will get a thick layer of cream on the top of the milk.

- Take a clean Pearl Pet jar of 1 kg. size. Add $\frac{1}{4}$ cup curd at the bottom and keep adding your daily cream to it until the bottle is full.

- Boil the cream with betel nut leaves as described above, cook the cream and strain the melted ghee into a clean bottle.